FROM TRACKWAYS TO MOTORWAYS
5000 Years of Highway History

FROM TRACKWAYS TO MOTORWAYS
5000 Years of Highway History

Hugh Davies

TEMPUS

First published 2006

Tempus Publishing Limited
The Mill, Brimscombe Port,
Stroud, Gloucestershire, GL5 2QG
www.tempus-publishing.com

© Hugh Davies, 2006

The right of Hugh Davies to be identified as the Author
of this work has been asserted in accordance with the
Copyrights, Designs and Patents Act 1988.

All rights reserved. No part of this book may be reprinted
or reproduced or utilised in any form or by any electronic,
mechanical or other means, now known or hereafter invented,
including photocopying and recording, or in any information
storage or retrieval system, without the permission in writing
from the Publishers.

British Library Cataloguing in Publication Data.
A catalogue record for this book is available from the British Library.

ISBN 0 7524 3650 3

Typesetting and origination by Tempus Publishing Limited
Printed in Great Britain

CONTENTS

List of tables and illustrations					7
Acknowledgements					11
Preface					13

1 Introduction					15
2 The first road-builders: separating facts from myths					19
3 Roman roads to motor roads: our modern network emerges					39
4 Structure of roads and tracks					75
5 The shape of roads					105
6 Using the roads					125
7 Conclusions and speculations					153

Bibliography					165
Appendix: chronological list of events					171
Index					187

LIST OF TABLES AND ILLUSTRATIONS

TABLES

Table 1 Relationship between soil type, drainage, traffic level and construction depth
Table 2 The total length of different categories of road
Table 3 Chronological list of significant events in the history of roads

ILLUSTRATIONS

1 The line of the Devil's Highway Roman road at Crowthorne, Berkshire
2 View from the M6 motorway as it passes through the Cumbrian Hills
3 Artist's view of the Bronze Age timber trackway at Bramcote Green, Bermondsey
4 Preserved timbers of the Bronze Age causeway at Flag Fen, Norfolk
5 Half-scale reconstruction of the Bronze Age causeway at Flag Fen, Norfolk
6 Bronze Age droveway at Flag Fen, Norfolk
7 Artist's reconstruction of the Bronze Age settlement and droveway at Hornchurch, Essex
8 Plot of Iron Age finds from Danebury hillfort, Wiltshire

FROM TRACKWAYS TO MOTORWAYS: 5000 YEARS OF HIGHWAY HISTORY

9   Hilaire Belloc's drawing of Roman roads and ridgeways
10 The Great Ridgeway, near Uffington Castle hillfort, Berkshire
11 *Scema Britannie*, thirteenth-century map drawn by Matthew Paris
12 Principal Roman roads in Britain
13 Suggested course of early Roman roads in Britain
14 Reconstruction drawing of a street in Roman Silchester
15 Line of the Roman road along the Gask Ridge, near Perth and Kinross
16 Roman Dere Street, near Jedburgh, Borders (Scottish)
17 Primary and secondary roads, shown on the fourteenth-century Gough Map
18 Bridge over the river Welland, at Stamford, Lincolnshire
19 The A6 road at Shap Fell, Cumbria
20 The extent of the turnpike road system in 1750
21 Abandoned turnpike road at Puddlehill, Hertfordshire
22 Changes in journey times, 1660-1810
23 High Street, Abington, Lanarkshire, *c.*1910
24 High Street, Abington, Lanarkshire, 2005
25 Enclosure map of North and South Killingholme, Lincolnshire
26 Extent of the eighteenth-century military road system in the Highlands of Scotland
27 Devil's Staircase, part of the military road network near Glencoe, Highland Region
28 Devil's Staircase, near Glencoe, Highland Region, showing a cross-drain
29 Balaculish Bridge, over Loch Leven, Highland Region
30 View from Balaculish Bridge, over Loch Leven, Highland Region
31 Military road, west of Kinghouse, above modern A82, Highland Region
32 Thomas Telford's Menai Bridge, Anglesey
33 Telford's Holyhead Road, now the A5, near Lake Ogwen, Conway
34 Second view of Telford's Holyhead Road, near Lake Ogwen, Conway
35 The motorway network in 1978
36 The M74 motorway near Abington, Lanarkshire
37 Artist's impression of an urban area, redeveloped to give maximum access to cars
38 Diagram showing layers of metalling in an asphalt road
39 Diagram showing typical form of Roman road metalling
40 Excavated surface of Roman Stane Street, at Westhampnett, near Chichester, West Sussex
41 Cross-section drawing of road layers at the site of St George's Street Roman baths, Canterbury, Kent
42 Modern planing/scarifying machine, removing worn-out road layers

LIST OF TABLES AND ILLUSTRATIONS

43 Reconstruction of Middleton Road, Manchester, in 1948
44 Barber-Greene carpeting machine, at Middleton Road, Manchester, in 1948
45 Laying of asphalt road surface at Middleton Road, Manchester, in 1918
46 Diagram showing engineered and un-engineered minor roads
47 Major reconstruction work at Sandhurst, Berkshire, 2005
48 Laying of adhesion mats between road layers at Sandhurst, Berkshire
49 Bridge over river Thames at Abingdon, Oxfordshire
50 View of one arch of Abingdon Bridge, Oxfordshire
51 Complex of bridges at Berwyn, near Llangollen, Denbighshire
52 Sixteenth-century bridge over river Dee, near Trevor, Denbighshire
53 The A5 trunk road, passing through the deep cutting at Puddlehill, Hertfordshire
54 The effect of gradient on horse-drawn vehicles
55 Work in progress, in 1925/6, to reduce gradient on the Llanfair Talhaiarn – Llansaran road, Conway
56 Dangerous section of A68 road, north of Corbridge, Northumberland
57 Diagram of a transition curve
58 A straight section of M1 motorway in Hertfordshire
59 A continuously curved section of M4 motorway in Berkshire
60 Section of an Autobahn in Germany, 1938
61 Diagram showing six designs for grade-separated junctions
62 Early zebra crossing, c.1951
63 A Street Audit in Bakewell, Derbyshire
64 Pedestrians on Holland Park Avenue, Notting Hill, London
65 Passenger and freight movements in South Hampshire, between 1770 and 1850
66 The number of horse-drawn and motor vehicle licences, issued between 1900 and 1940
67 The number of motor vehicle licences issued between 1900 and 2000
68 Cyclists on Devil's Highway Roman road, Crowthorne, Berkshire
69 Opening of the first section of the National Cycling Network in 1984
70 The number of commercial vehicle licences issued between 1900 and 2000
71 Commercial vehicle weight limits between 1900 and 2000
72 Annual fatalities on Britain's roads, between 1870 and 1900
73 Elborough Street, South London, c.1900
74 Elborough Street, South London, c.2000
75 A memorable encounter during a walk through the woods

ACKNOWLEDGEMENTS

I would like to thank Sally Stow, Robert Huxford, Ray Laurence, Brian Kemp, Michael Fulford and Martin Bell for their help and encouragement during research for this book. All photographs, maps and diagrams are copyright to Hugh Davies, unless otherwise specified. I am most grateful to the following people and organisations for permission to use images for which they hold the copyright: Sophie Lamb, Museum of London (Bramcote timber trackway); Barry Cunliffe and Council for British Archaeology (Iron Age finds at Danebury); David Yates (reconstruction drawing of droveway); David Yates, Greg Priestly-Bell, Archaeology South-East (excavation of Stane Street, near Chichester); Margaret Matthews and Silchester Town Life Project (reconstruction drawing, Silchester street); British Library (*Scema Britannie* by Matthew Paris); Jane Elder, Canterbury Archaeological Trust (excavation at St George's Street bathhouse); Elsevier Publishing (extent of turnpike network, reduction in travel times and motorway network); Duncan MacBride and Biggar Museum (High Street, Abington); Rex Russell, Paul Hindle and Phillimore Publishing (Enclosure map of Killingholme); Georgina Hobhouse, House of Lochar Publishing (map of military roads); Office of Public Sector Information (formerly HMSO) and Department for Transport (reconstruction drawing of urban development); University College, Lampeter (cross-sections of minor roads); Hester Brown, Living Streets (street audit and early zebra); Jonathan Bewley, SUSTRANS (opening of first section of the National Cycle Network); Robert Huxford and Michael Chrimes, Institution of Civil Engineers (ICE) (German Autobahn, roadworks at Middleton Road, Manchester and on Llanfair Talhaiarn – Llansaran road, Conway. Also, Elborough Road, London, 1900 and 2000); Ron Bridle, John Porter, Thomas Telford Publishing and ICE (diagrams of transition curves and junction designs); Maurice White, Quarry Products Association (diagram of road layers).

I am also grateful to Peter Kemmis Betty, Laura Perehinec, Tom Sunley and other colleagues at Tempus Publishing for their help and advice during the publication of this book.

Finally may I pay tribute to my wife, Gillian, for all her help in picture-taking, proof-reading, checking of illustrations and numerous suggestions for improvements. This book is my own work, as the author, but the final product has benefited enormously from her contribution.

PREFACE

Having spent most of my professional career as a transport scientist, dealing with modern roads and traffic, it was an enjoyable retirement project to delve back in history to the Romans' occupation of Britain, in order to examine how the approach of these famous road-builders matches up to our modern engineering practice. In my book (Davies 2002) I showed that many of the features of Roman road design and construction are readily recognisable, and indeed are still followed. After all, the laws of nature have not changed; successful road-building has always required that the available technology and resources be harnessed to produce a route along which anyone can travel, across the land, between the start and finish of their journey.

So the obvious question arises: how did road-builders from other eras set about the same task? This book addresses that question, by looking at five millennia of British road-building and road-using, from the Mesolithic footprints found on the Severn Estuary (a do-it-yourself trackway) to modern motorways, streets and traffic. Along the way we shall encounter myths and legends about the origin of roads, extraordinary road-builders like Blind Jack of Knaresborough, intrepid travellers, battling against, and even relishing the hazards of journeying by road, and the experience and attitude of those who dwelt alongside them.

1

INTRODUCTION

Of all man-made artefacts, roads are perhaps the most extensive but least regarded. For example, walkers along a country lane have always admired the wild flowers growing alongside, while in the stage-coach era riders gazed out eagerly to spot the grand houses which they knew they would be passing. Yet the road they were travelling along remained almost unnoticed. Today, there is still much to enjoy as we walk or drive (*1*, *2*), but the road itself is still no more regarded than it ever was. Yet the history of our roads is a fascinating story. For thousands of years we have travelled overland; paths, tracks and roads developed to help us to do just that. How this came about in the past, and is continuing to do so today, is the subject of this book.

We start, in the next chapter, with some evidence of early tracks, dating from Mesolithic times, when hunter-gatherers moved from place to place in search of food. Some remarkable human footprints have been found in river estuaries, such as that of the Severn, which date from this period. As we move to the Neolithic, with the beginning of a more settled lifestyle, based on farming, we find traces of tracks leading to fields and pastures. In very wet areas, the remains of timber trackways have been found, built to link together small islands of habitable land surrounded by marsh or wetlands. Though the Romans were the first to use metalling to any large extent, there are some signs of it from the Iron Age, mainly linked to concentrated settlements on hillforts.

FROM TRACKWAYS TO MOTORWAYS: 5000 YEARS OF HIGHWAY HISTORY

1 A public footpath at Crowthorne, Berkshire; though nowadays only a minor track through the woods, 2000 years ago it lay on the major Roman road running west from Londinium

We then consider cases where myth and legend is often as important as any physical evidence. Examples such as the Ridgeways, the 'Royal Roads' and 'Helen's Roads' and even ley lines, all hark back to an imagined past when our forebears criss-crossed the whole of Britain along grand, strategic routes.

INTRODUCTION

2 View from the M6, northbound, as it passes through the Cumbrian Hills

There now follow four chapters which look at different aspects, of road history; destination, structure, shape and use. Chapter 3 discusses how our modern network emerged from the Roman and medieval periods to the present day. The Romans seemed to have had a strategic vision of how roads should be laid out across the island of *Britannia*; their roads provided direct links between distant places. Anglo-Saxon and Norse successors had a more local requirement, adapting or losing altogether the Roman inheritance. It was this local network, with only occasional Roman antecedents, which gradually formed itself into what we know today. Finally, we can see our motorways as bringing back to Britain a strategic approach to road-building.

In Chapter 4 we look at an aspect of a road which is hard to appreciate until something goes wrong, namely its structure. If a road is not strong enough to carry the traffic which wishes to use it, it quickly cracks, crumbles and ultimately becomes impassable. But even when a road is adequate for a given level of traffic, it can fail when traffic volumes, or vehicle weights increase, as they have tended to do. The history of road-building is a continuous struggle to make ever-stronger roads to keep up with this demand. Besides looking at the technical aspects of this struggle, we shall encounter some of the famous and sometimes colourful characters who have made contributions. We shall also encounter the deleterious effects of rising street levels, and the chapter ends with a section on the history of bridges, and their contribution to the reliability of the road network.

While the *structure* of a road may be hard to appreciate, its *shape* is far more obvious. Chapter 5 looks at this aspect, comprising elements such as gradient, curvature and cross-section. As with road structure, these features are intimately bound up with the traffic which the road is designed to carry, though in this case it is the speed, capacity and safety of road users which are determining factors, rather than whether or not the road is strong enough.

Chapter 6 covers use of roads; what they are like is inextricably bound up with the way they are used. Though the two go together, it has usually been the case that changing habits of use have forced road-builders to improve their methods and designs to cope with new situations. We shall look at various modes of travel, such as walking, riding on horseback and travelling in a coach, and also at the haulage of goods by pack animal or wagon. Then we move on to the rise of motor vehicles, powered by steam, petrol or diesel, and not forgetting the rise and decline of the pedal cycle. We shall also look at how the risk of death has changed since before the motor era, and how our attitudes to roads and traffic change over time.

Chapter 7 takes a look ahead and assesses what the lessons of history can tell us about the future of roads. As we shall see the main problem is likely to be matching our aspirations and expectations of ever increasing travel opportunities with the rather less impressive reality of what is possible. Even if the road is still there to carry us to our destination, will we be able to use it in the free-wheeling manner we have become accustomed to?

In the Appendix can be found a chronological list of some of the main events in the history of roads, including the main Parliamentary Statutes and Regulations which have been introduced to control traffic.

2

THE FIRST ROAD-BUILDERS: SEPARATING FACTS FROM MYTHS

INTRODUCTION

In this chapter we start by looking back to the Mesolithic, not long after the end of the last Ice Age. These early hunter-gatherers left footprints on the shores of river estuaries which have been preserved, enabling us to begin the story of our road history with traces of actual journey-making. There were no formal roads, or even tracks, at this stage, but it was not too long, as a more settled lifestyle began to take shape in the Neolithic, before identifiable tracks, marked by ditches, can be seen; these were probably used for driving animals to pasture or markets. We shall also discuss timber trackways, in marshy areas, as well as the very first examples of the use of stone *metalling*, to avoid well-used tracks becoming too churned up and muddy. It is archaeology which enables us to see this picture of an emerging network of essentially local tracks, serving the needs of a local, mainly agricultural economy. But, for some, this picture is too limited. They prefer to see, in prehistoric times, the existence of a highly developed civilisation who surveyed and laid out a strategic network of straight roads, marked even today by *ley lines*. Their evidence is not archaeological, but observational; they claim to see patterns everywhere and build their theories accordingly. As we shall see, harking back to an ancient tradition of road-building has itself a long tradition, stretching back to Norman times or even earlier, with the 'Four Royal Roads' and 'Helen's Roads'. Thus, rather implausibly, roads are made into symbols of a fondly imagined, 'lost' civilisation. The same idea seems to be at work when the Ridgeways are described as 'our oldest roads'; yet even these may not be as old as they seem, but are the creation of Victorian antiquarians, who had an equally romantic vision of antiquity.

EVIDENCE FOR PREHISTORIC TRACKS

Mesolithic footprints

Walking is the way people have travelled overland for the vast majority of human history. People walked in Britain before the last Ice Age, 10,000 years ago, and returned when the ice retreated. While the presence of prehistoric people can be traced by the artefacts they produced, used and discarded, and, later, by the timber trackways they built in waterlogged areas (see below), one would hardly expect to see direct evidence of any one of the countless journeys people made on foot. Yet, because of the way some of our river estuaries have developed since the last Ice Age, human footprints from the Mesolithic period have been found and recorded. A particularly fruitful area has been along the inter-tidal shores of the River Severn, south of Newport, Gwent, at Uskmouth, Magor Pill and Goldcliff (Aldhouse-Green 1992; Scales 2002). A set of such footprints was found near Goldcliff, one of which had been made by a 3-year-old child, who was apparently accompanying an adult as they walked inland from the estuary.

These tracks can be dated by dendrochronology to about 4500 BC, towards the end of the Mesolithic period. Hunting and gathering was the main means of providing food, and it seems likely that most of the activity on the foreshore was concerned with fishing. Finding and recording these prints involves specialised knowledge and the rapid deployment of refined techniques; for example, the tracks at Goldcliff are only exposed for a maximum of just over two hours at low tide.

These tracks are highly evocative because they record particular journeys. No doubt to the people who made the tracks there was nothing special about their walk along the shore that day, but to us they can be regarded as very special indeed; an improbable set of circumstances led to their footprints being gently filled in by deposits from rising water levels (deposits which were sufficiently different to distinguish them from the base layer on which the people had walked), then preserved beneath further layers, only to be gradually exposed again by more recent erosion. As a result we now have perhaps our earliest direct evidence of a journey on foot.

The origin of more permanent trackways

As people move about the land, they tend to follow a path which they, or others, have used earlier, though, often, these are hardly more than beaten earth. Ideas vary about how such early tracks originally formed. We examine some of the wilder ideas, such as ley lines, later in this chapter. A rather more plausible suggestion is made by Hilaire Belloc, who imagines early man trying out different routes across an area of hills and rivers, seeking the most direct and convenient alternative by a process of trial and error (Belloc 1924). Christopher Taylor's ideas are rather more evolutionary; he suggests that tracks were first based on the routes selected by the animals which our early ancestors hunted, gradually becoming accepted as a convenient route for general travel (Taylor 1979, 2).

Timber trackways

Apart from the Mesolithic footprints, some of the oldest-known travel routes comprise timber trackways through wet or marshy areas, or those subject to regular flooding such as the Somerset Levels. Timbers have survived in the waterlogged ground, enabling both the construction method and the exact date of felling to be established. Some of these date from the Neolithic period, such as the Sweet Track, which was constructed about 4000 BC, and was regularly maintained (Coles and Coles 1986, 56). But the technique continued to be used, with variations, throughout the Bronze and Iron Ages. For example, two phases of trackway-building were found near the Thames, at Bramcote Green, Bermondsey, dating to about 1500 BC (Thomas and Rackham 1996). Phase I used two parallel lines of alder logs, laid longitudinally on the surface of the marsh, sometimes being pinned in position by vertical pegs. In Phase II, oak logs were used instead, but, perhaps because they were more difficult to handle than alder, or needed to be transported further, only a single line was laid (3).

Other examples of pre-Roman timber trackways have been found; at Greenwich 300yds east of the Thames, layers of wooden stakes date from 1600-1300 BC (Philip and Garrod 1994), while on the west bank of the Severn estuary at Goldcliff, a timber trackway was made of reused boat planks dating to 1170 BC (Bell et al. 2000, 82).

The most likely purpose of these trackways was to provide every day access on foot to settlements which would otherwise have been unreachable except by boat; for example, there is evidence of settlements near each end of the trackway at Bramcote Green, Bermondsey, referred to above. A site such as Flag Fen, near Peterborough, which seems to be associated mainly with ceremonial functions, may also have had a timber trackway to access it, though the extensive line of posts which has already been found may have had other functions, besides giving support to a trackway (Pryor 1991, 121) (4, 5).

3 Artist's impression of Phase II of a Bronze Age timber trackway at Bramcote Green, Bermondsey, on waterlogged ground in the Thames valley. After Thomas and Rakham 1996, figure 23

Of course, these trackways are of great interest because of their age and level of preservation. However, they are probably exceptional because of their unusual environment; some technology was needed to facilitate ready movement through the waterlogged areas in which they were built. Yet, as we see below, there is little evidence that any form of technology was applied to road-making generally during prehistory. While there is a possibility that examples have been missed, the most likely explanation is that there was no great need for it. These tracks demonstrate that, where people could not move about as they wished without the application of technology, our ancient ancestors were quite capable of providing it.

Local tracks

Most of Britain is not subject to the permanent or seasonal waterlogging which necessitated the building of timber trackways in the Somerset Levels and other wetland areas. Elsewhere, tracks were often no more than regularly used pathways through settlements, fields and common areas, used mainly for local journeys. Their lack of structure makes them difficult to identify. However, regular use can cause the ground to be worn down into a hollow, producing what are known as hollow-ways; once formed these can remain in use for long periods, and the poor drainage makes the soil within soft, so accelerating the rate of formation. However, many hollow-ways formed during the Anglo-Saxon and medieval periods, so dating can be a problem, but their longevity often makes them visible on aerial photographs. Even when the ground has not been worn into hollow-ways it is

THE FIRST ROAD-BUILDERS: SEPARATING FACTS FROM MYTHS

Above: 4 Collapsed timbers of a short section of a massive Bronze Age causeway found at Flag Fen, Norfolk. They are preserved, in the position in which they were found, by being regularly sprayed with water

Below: 5 A half-scale reconstruction of the Bronze Age causeway found at Flag Fen

possible to identify trackways from the parallel ditches which were sometimes dug alongside them, to provide drainage, to mark out boundaries, or simply to discourage animals from straying. These ditches can appear as crop-marks on aerial photographs, though Taylor has pointed out the limitations of relying on this technique; he describes a site at Owselbury, near Winchester, where aerial survey seemed to show a straightforward pattern of trackways leading across contemporary fields to an Iron Age farm. However, excavation revealed a highly complex picture, with tracks coming into use and being abandoned from the early Iron Age to well into the Roman period, and one trackway which continued in use until the nineteenth century (Taylor 1979, 24).

A particular form of track, used primarily for moving animals, is called a drove or droveway. In medieval times these were often long-distance routes, without formal boundaries, which were used to bring animals from the country areas,

6 A Bronze Age droveway at Flag Fen, with flanking ditches marked by the vegetation on each side

where they were reared, to the large markets which grew up as towns expanded. However, the term is also used for much more local tracks, within a particular field system, where deep ditches were used to prevent animals from straying off the intended route. Many of these are of ancient date: for example, Bronze Age droveways have been found at Fengate, near Peterborough (Pryor 1991, 54-62) and South Hornchurch, Essex (Guttmann and Last 2000) (6, 7). It may be that the latter example is part of a wider network, linking regional markets (Yates, forthcoming).

Sometimes tracks can be inferred because of the *lack* of evidence. This is particularly likely where occupation is quite dense; the presence of buildings, storage pits, waste dumps etc. leave readily located evidence, while the paths, tracks or roads which pass between these sites have little or no discarded items on them. A good example has been found at Danebury, an Iron Age hillfort in Hampshire.

7 Artist's view of the Bronze Age settlement at South Hornchurch, Essex, showing a well-used droveway. *Casper Johnson; after Yates, forthcoming*

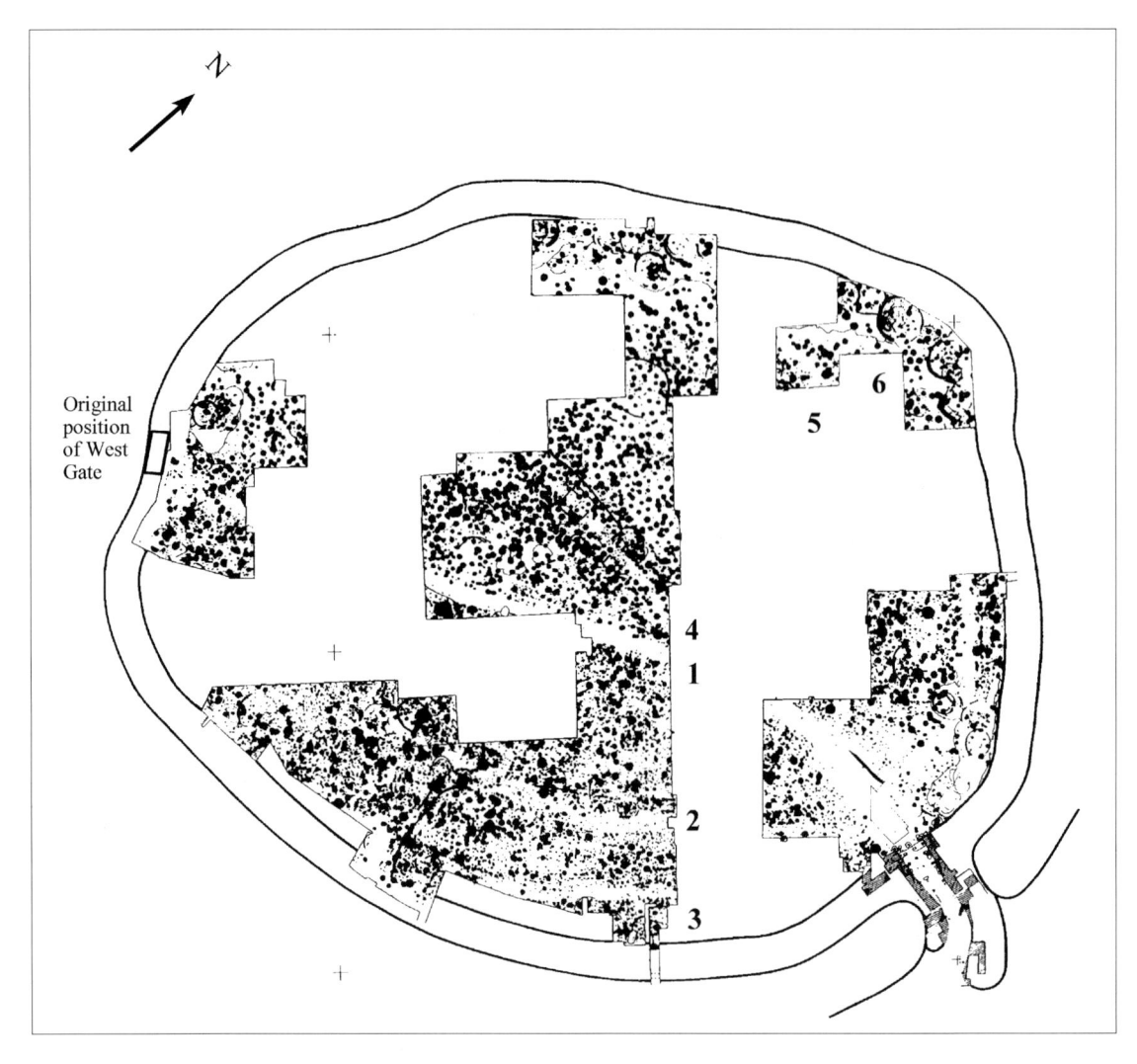

8 Plot of all Iron Age finds from excavations at Danebury hillfort. After Cunliffe 1995, figure 6

Barry Cunliffe and his team excavated the defended area at the summit for over a decade during the 1980s; they showed that there had been occupation for over four centuries. When the Iron Age finds from these excavations were plotted, some linear gaps could be discerned which were interpreted as a series of roads through the settlement (*8*). Road One may have predated the hillfort settlement and seems to have determined the position of the gateways on the east and west sides. This latter gateway was later blocked, but the road remained the principal spine. There was some metalling (see below), formed with small pieces of chalk, but most of the pattern of trackways in the settlement can only be inferred from the lack of finds (Cunliffe 1995, 42). It appears that they were kept reasonably clear of debris, and were not used as dumps for waste material, as happened to the streets in some medieval towns.

The use of metalling

Metalling, comprising layers of stone in road construction, is needed to protect the underlying soil from damage arising from heavy traffic, particularly wheeled vehicles. It is usually associated with the Romans, and was not used widely again in Britain until the post-medieval period. Its use in prehistory seems also to have been very limited; the vast majority of excavations of prehistoric sites which include evidence of trackways make no reference to any trace of metalling. However, there may be exceptions.

We refer above to the excavations at Danebury, which have revealed a series of roads through the hillfort settlement. Some metalling, comprising chalk cobbles, has been found on Road One as it passed through the west gate, before this was blocked. The remainder of Road One, and most other roads do not seem to have been regularly metalled, receiving only occasional patching. An unexplained exception is Road Two, which received several layers of metalling (Cunliffe 1991, 152).

At Silchester traces of a pre-Roman street grid, laid out on a north-east/south-west alignment (in contrast to the north–south/east–west alignment of the Roman grid), have been found beneath the forum/basilica (Fulford and Timby 2000, 26-8). Though precise dating is not possible, these early streets appear to have been laid down during the period 15 BC to AD 40-50. They can usually be traced by noting the presence of parallel ditches with an absence of finds between them, but parts of at least two streets appear to have had a metalled surface of cobbles. This may suggest that the Iron Age settlement had developed to such an extent that traffic, whether pedestrian, animal or wheeled, had become sufficiently dense so as to merit such treatment to avoid the street becoming impassably muddy and churned up. More evidence for this early street metalling is being revealed by the on-going excavation at Insula IX, by Reading University (www.silchester.reading.ac.uk).

Another example, in Ireland, has recently been announced, though not yet formally reported (*British Archaeology* March 2003, 7; *Current Archaeology* December 2004). The site, at Corrstown in Co. Londonderry, is of Bronze Age date, and comprised a 10yds-wide main street of a settlement, flanked by 29 roundhouses, linked to the street by pathways and side-streets. All the streets and paths seem to have had some form of stone metalling, such as cobbles or flagstones. If this finding is confirmed in a formal report it will be a startling exception to what is currently known about such early settlements.

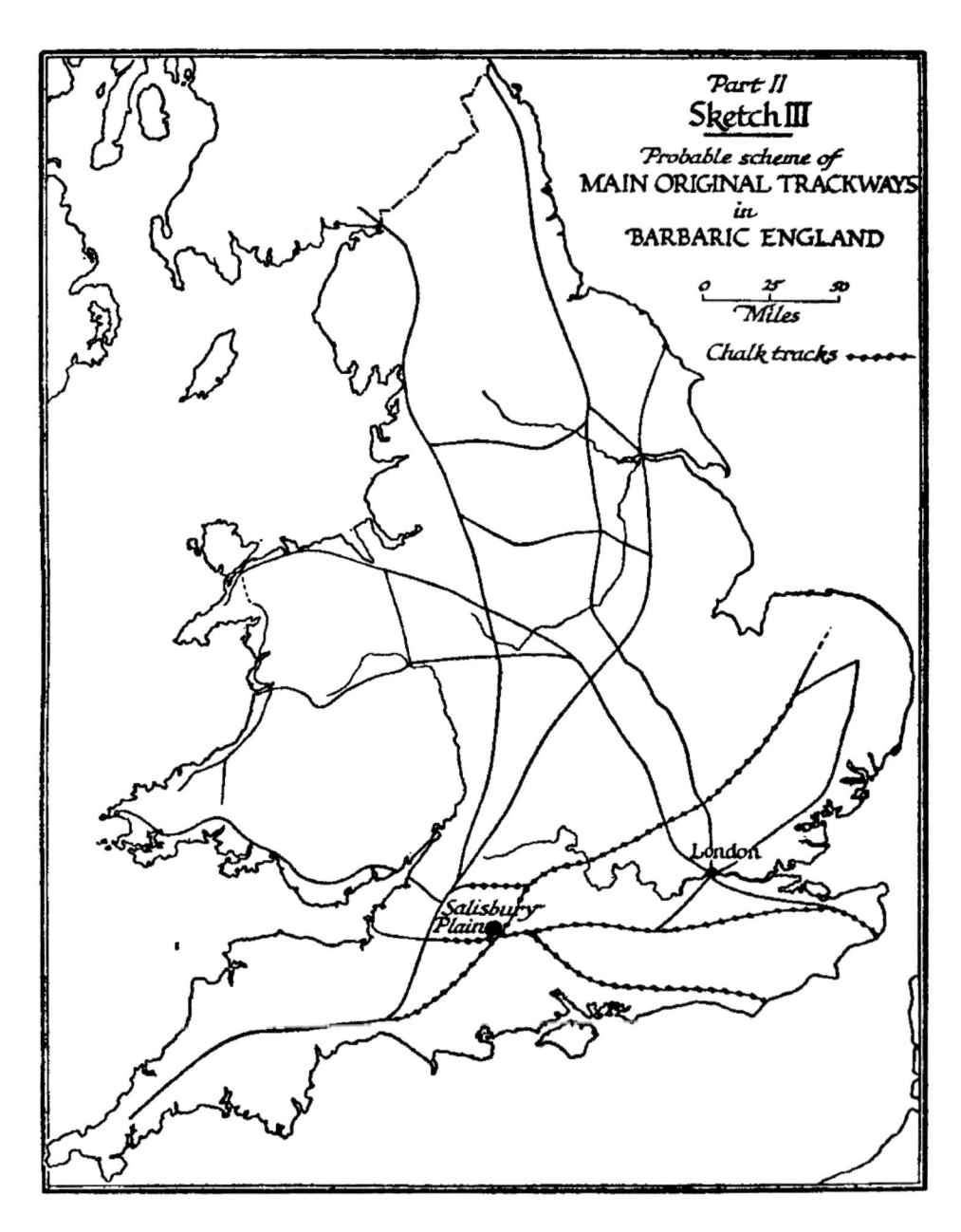

9 Roman roads (solid lines) and ridgeways (hatched lines). *After Belloc 1924, 118*

THE RIDGEWAYS: ARE THEY REALLY OUR OLDEST ROADS?

Introduction
In 1924 Hilaire Belloc published a book called *The Road* in which he describes the way roads have developed (9). He believed that the Romans built their roads along trackways which had been established shortly before their invasion (shown by the solid lines), but he considered that the earliest long-distance tracks in Britain were those which followed the various chalk and limestone chains of hills (shown by the hatched lines). These have come to be known as the Ridgeways, and Belloc is far from being alone in considering them to be of early prehistoric origin; in fact it is the prevalent view of those who write about them today. Yet this view is being increasingly challenged by archaeologists, who are now suggesting that the supposed longevity of these tracks owes more to seventeenth- and eighteenth-century antiquarian enthusiasm than to hard physical evidence. We explore some of these ideas below.

What are the Ridgeways and where do they go?
The ridges of hills are often designated as downs, or downland, and Belloc identified seven routes which followed them, all radiating roughly from Salisbury Plain: the first followed the Dorset Downs, south-west to the Dorset coast, the second followed variants of the same hills to Southampton Water; then came a third following the Hampshire and Sussex Downs to the Sussex coast, the fourth followed the North Downs to Canterbury and Dover, the fifth went along the Berkshire Downs and then the Chiltern Hills, ending on the Norfolk Coast near the Wash, the sixth went westward to the Mendips and the seventh followed the Cotswold Ridge in a north-easterly direction (this last he depicts as a Roman road, though describing it as a ridgeway). Nearly all of these are now well-signed, preserved pathways, though there is confusion about their names, and sometimes their courses. Perhaps the most straightforward description is given by T.G. Millar, who calls the route to the Sussex coast (Belloc's third) the South Downs Way, starting at Winchester and ending at Eastbourne; while the route to Canterbury (Belloc's fourth) is called the North Downs Way, starting at Farnham and ending at Dover and Folkestone (Millar 1977, 106). Some other authors show these two, respectively, as the South and North Hants Ridgeways (Timperley and Brill 2005, 6; Hindle 2001, 3), while the latter is often called the Pilgrim's Way, which, by including a short link from Winchester to Farnham, can be suggested as the route for pilgrims visiting Thomas Becket's shrine at Canterbury (Wright 1971). Belloc was somewhat hesitant about his seventh route, along the Cotswolds, but subsequently this line was given prominence by W.G. Grimes, who named it the Jurassic Way, running from the Devon coast to the Wash (Grimes 1951).

10 The Great Ridgeway, viewed from Uffington hillfort, heading westward

Perhaps the most famous of these routes does not really have a name at all, other than The Ridgeway, The Great Ridgeway, or The Ridgeway Path (*10*). Hindle has it starting on the Dorset coast, as does Belloc's first route (Hindle 2001, 3), though most writers have it commencing near Avebury (Belloc's fifth). It passes in a northerly direction just east of Avebury, before turning more to the east, passing the Uffington White Horse, to reach the Thames at Goring. During most of this latter section, from Wanborough onwards, it is parallelled by another route, the Icknield Way, which runs somewhat to the north, though rejoining the Ridgeway at Goring. It is now conventional to name the continuation of the Ridgeway into East Anglia as Icknield Way (one of the Four Royal Roads, see below), which gradually turns north to reach the Norfolk coast at Holme. Much of the route of Icknield Way in Norfolk is thought to have been made or modified by the Romans and is usually included in any list of Roman roads (Margary 1973, 262; Davies 2002, 171).

The oldest roads?

Belloc does not give a suggested date for the origin of the ridgeways, but gives a reasonable rationale for why they can be claimed to be our oldest roads. He points out that the chalk downlands provide a well-drained surface, well suited for walking upon, while the linear arrangement of hills provided an efficient course and guide for travellers. His caution is not shared by most writers, who use descriptions such as 'Britain's oldest road', or even 'The oldest road in Europe' (Anderson and Godwin 1975, 180). Walkers along the well-signposted routes of many of the ridgeways can be forgiven for thinking they are treading in the footsteps of their ancient forebears. It is sometimes claimed that these formed the routes for trade, immigration or invasion, while the apparent focus of many of these routes on Salisbury Plain has allowed the assumption that they were used by Neolithic and Bronze Age people, hurrying from far afield to attend important festivals at Stonehenge and Avebury (Wright 1971, 12).

Yet all this is almost certainly an illusion. The first problem is that ancient trackways were not neatly confined to well-fenced courses, but were composed of numerous, alternative paths, which might spread over more than a mile (1.6km) wide area of ground, as people picked their way along unprepared land. It was only with the eighteenth-century enclosure movement that most areas were fenced off, leaving roads and tracks well defined. If these ridgeways are of ancient origin, we need to think of a broad swathe rather than a narrow path.

The second problem arises when archaeologists look for some dateable evidence. Perhaps the first to dent the comfortable image of these ancient pathways was Christopher Taylor, who in 1979 questioned the credentials of both the Jurassic and Icknield Ways (Taylor 1979, 32ff). Proponents of Neolithic or Bronze Age dates for these routes used the preponderance of settlements of this time along the uplands of chalk and limestone hills. But Taylor shows that, when all the settlement evidence is gathered, there is no tendency to cluster along these routes; far from preferring to live on the higher ground, away from the supposed dangers of the forested valleys, prehistoric inhabitants settled right across the landscape. Thus, even if there was an ancient trackway, settlement evidence gave no clue as to where it lay. More recently Sarah Harrison has shown that a set of earthworks called the Cambridgeshire Dykes, which straddle the presumed lines of Icknield Way, date from the fifth or sixth centuries AD, yet show no gaps through which such an important route would need to pass (Harrison, S. 2004, 13). Even the assumed prehistoric age of the Ridgeway itself has been assailed. Peter Fowler has studied the parishes of Overton and Fyfield, through which the Ridgeway passes, a short distance to the east of Avebury in Wiltshire. He shows that there are prehistoric and Roman field systems in the area, both of which are overlain by the Ridgeway itself (Fowler 1998, 31). He concludes that this particular trackway is one of the more recent additions to the landscape in this area.

Even the notion of long-distance trading routes in prehistory (a popular argument for the existence of ridgeways) has been questioned. Most trading was done on the basis of individual barter transactions, so that any particular object would move across the landscape in a series of random stages, as it was repeatedly exchanged, hand to hand. Grahame Clark has emphasised the exchange of valuable items such as axes or adzes on the basis of reinforcing kinship obligations, rather than trade for profit (Clark 1965), while Mark Edmonds points out that, for any particular item, the whole process could take generations (Edmonds 1995, 51). Sarah Harrison, in questioning the antiquity of the Icknield Way, quotes B. Orme's remark that 'artefacts moved further than people' (Harrison, S. 2004, 6). Thus there does not appear to have been a nationwide trading system in the Stone Age, and therefore no demand for a nationwide network of trade routes to service it. This still leaves open the question of how it is that there is such a widespread belief that the ridgeways provided just such a network, a question we address below.

A centuries-old idea of millennia-old roads

So if the ridgeways are not prehistoric, how old are they? As we have seen there is serious doubt about whether these tracks were prehistoric, and for the most part they do not seem to be Roman either. Even in the Anglo-Saxon period it is hard to find evidence for their use as long-distance routes, and though the term 'ridgeway' seems to be over a thousand years old, it is not applied to significant lengths of trackway. There are no ridgeways on the Gough Map, *c.*1350 (see next chapter, under Roman to medieval), but they do gradually start to appear on later map books and series, and are often shown on early Ordnance Survey maps of the nineteenth century. What seems to have happened is that the ridgeways are the outcome of an *idea* of what ancient Britain was like, promoted by Victorian and earlier antiquarians, keen to reconstruct a communication system worthy of those who built such dramatic monuments as Stonehenge and Avebury. The fact that lines of hills seem to point towards these monuments from all points of the compass, was too good a clue to what went on in prehistory to ignore. We have inherited this notion, and cemented it in the preservation and promotion of some magnificent long-distance paths. The suggestion that evidence for their prehistoric origin is flimsy need not detract from the enjoyment of using them; after all, their existence is part of our history, even though evidence for their use as a means of reaching Stonehenge from far-flung parts of the island is no more secure than the idea that the monument was built by the Druids.

SOME MORE ROAD-MAKING MYTHS

The Four Royal Roads

In the middle years of the thirteenth century a monk at the Abbey of St Albans, called Matthew Paris, drew up a large number of maps, showing various parts of the pilgrim route to Palestine. Most of these maps, including several of Britain, depict the route as a series of place-names; thus we would describe these as *itinerary maps*, in which the course of the road is not shown explicitly, but is inferred from the names of places along it. However, he did produce one map, known as the *Scema Britannie*, comprising a map of Britain with four roads marked on it (*11*). The map is not highly regarded by historians of cartography, probably because the outline of the coast is very crude and few places are marked on it. But as a contribution to the history of roads in Britain it is significant because it is probably the earliest medieval map to show roads explicitly. However, it is significant from another point of view too, because of which roads are shown and the course they take.

The map, with west at the top, shows four roads, Watling Street, Foss Way, Icknield Street and Ermine Street; these roads are referred to in the Laws of Edward the Confessor, a compilation of current statutes brought together shortly after the Normal Conquest. These particular roads are described as carrying special royal status, namely that travellers along them were protected against harm by the King's Peace; thus they have come to be known as the Four Royal Roads. The course of these roads is not specified in the Laws, but their names are clearly identifiable as the Anglo-Saxon names of four prominent Roman roads. The next chapter deals with the development of this network in Roman times, and its subsequent history; for now the main interest is in the status these four particular roads acquired in the medieval period, both as a means of defining the land of Britain and as evidence of an ancient and glorious civilisation.

Matthew Paris showed the four roads thus: Icknield Street (Old Sarum to Bury St Edmunds); Foss Way (Totnes to Caithness); Watling Street (Dover to Chester); Ermine Street (south coast to north coast). They all cross at Dunstable; it is only because his depiction of the coastline is so distorted that Matthew Paris is able to make the four roads cross at a single point: these roads do not actually cross at one point. Even so, he does give the approximate orientation of the four roads, so what was his purpose?

A clue may lie in the references to the Royal Roads by several late medieval historians such as Henry of Huntingdon, Geoffrey of Monmouth and Ranulph Higden; their writing on this topic was reviewed in the nineteenth century by Edwin Guest (Guest 1857). They do not always agree about the precise course of the roads; for example, some have Watling Street or Icknield Street continuing into Wales, but they are all agreed about the names, that they straddle the island,

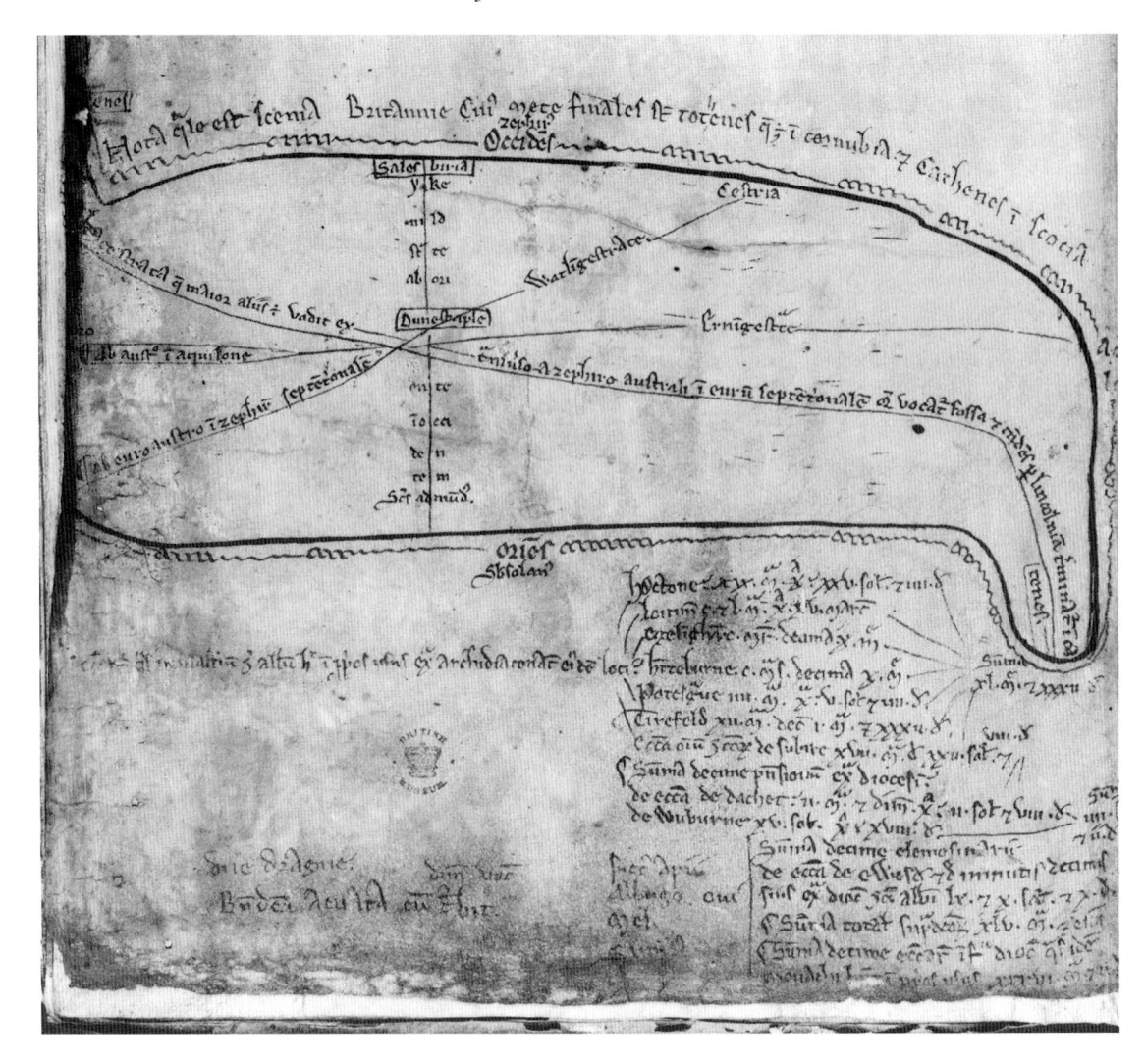

11 The Scema Britannie, drawn up by the thirteenth-century monk Matthew Paris. Courtesy British Library

and that they were built long before the Roman period. Usually they ascribe the builder as King Belinus, who is supposed to have reigned in the fourth century BC. Thus we can see these roads as symbolising both the extent of an ancient civilisation under one king, and its advanced development, to the extent that it was capable of building high-quality roads across the entire land. The identification of these roads perhaps also indicates the desire of the writers to see Britain as a unified country once more.

It seems fairly clear that the Four Royal Roads were in fact of Roman origin, but the suggestion that there were four dead-straight roads built in prehistoric times has not been lost on modern-day advocates of an advanced civilisation flourishing in Britain long before the arrival of the Romans. For example, John Michell sees these four roads as evidence for an extensive and accurate survey carried out by King Belinus, or his forebears, which used alignments and units which were related to the (accurately determined) dimensions of the earth (Michell 2004). In particular he assumes that Icknield Street is actually coincident with the so-called St Michael's ley line, running from Penzance to the Norfolk coast, so-called because it is said to pass through several places dedicated to St Michael.

The existence and status of these roads seems to continue to fascinate. But perhaps of more interest than where they actually went is whether or not the King's Peace meant anything in practice; did travellers favour one of these routes, always supposing they could be sure they were travelling along it, on the grounds that they would be safer than on alternatives? No evidence has been put forward on this topic, but the distinction became academic, when Henry I made the King's Peace applicable to all roads. We shall see in a later chapter what is known about travellers' safety in general.

The roads that Helen built

In Wales there is also a road-building legend, though in this case the historical setting is firmly in the Roman period. The Roman road running up the west coast of Wales is, by long tradition, called Sarn Helen (see the next chapter). The association of this name with road-building comes from the *Mabinogion*, a collection of Celtic folk tales, whose earliest, more or less complete, manuscript dates to 1325. However, these tales are probably based on earlier written versions, which themselves come from even earlier oral traditions (Gantz 1976, 9ff). They seem to relate to Britain during and shortly after the Roman period. Even when characters have some historic identity, their activities are portrayed in a visionary, dream-like style. One of the tales is entitled *The Dream of Maxen*, who is described as a Roman emperor and is most likely to be Magnus Maximus. Other sources show that, in AD 383, he was proclaimed emperor of Rome by the army under his control in Britain. He used these troops to make a successful, though short-lived bid for the emperorship, and the *Dream* relates many heroic deeds by the British contingent, under the command of a Welsh prince Kynan. Most of the tale is set while Maxen is in Britain, describing how he had a dream of seeing a young woman whom he sets out to find, and eventually weds. Her name was Helen, Kynan and Avaon's sister. However, something of the contorted structure of ancient Celtic tales can be gained from study of other texts which have Helen as a Welsh goddess, Constantine's mother Helena or even Helen of Troy (Bromwich 1961, 341ff). According to *The Dream of Maxen* Helen asks for three fortresses to be built for her, and later she 'thought to have highways built from one fortress to another across the island; these were built, and are now called the highways of Helen of the Hosts (*Elen Lluyddog*) because of her British origin – that is, because the men of the island would not have assembled for anyone else'. The fortresses appear to be Caernarfon, Carmarthen and Caerleon; there are certainly Roman roads between these, some at least of which carry the name Sarn Helen (Helen's Causeway); the road from near Caernarfon to Carmarthen carries this name, as does a branch to Llandovery, though not the rest of the route to Caerleon.

Whoever Helen was, and whatever her connection with road-building, her name lives on in the traditional name of at least some of the Roman roads in Wales; a tradition which might predate the naming and identifying of the Four Royal Roads referred to above.

Ley lines and the 'Old Straight Track'

On 30 June 1921 a prominent citizen of Hereford, aged 65, made an observation about the countryside near Bredwardine, between Hay-on-Wye and Hereford, which led to the creation of an entirely new category of landscape enthusiast, namely the 'ley-hunter'. For the rest of the century what happened that day led to an extraordinary variety of claims which took the whole business far beyond anything he could have imagined. The citizen in question was Alfred Watkins, businessman, local councillor, amateur photographer, inventor, naturalist and antiquarian. His interest and knowledge of the local area arose from his early work for his father's brewery business, travelling the area to visit the company's clients. On this fateful occasion he had been visiting friends and, while exploring the area on horseback he suddenly became aware that the prominent features he could see from his vantage point on high ground, such as churches, mounds, stone cairns, crossroads etc. seemed to lie in a series of straight lines. When, upon returning home, he studied maps of the area he became convinced that he was looking at a sophisticated network of straight alignments, delineated by a whole variety of prominent features in the landscape. He quickly devised a hypothesis that what he was seeing were the echoes of an ancient network of straight tracks, marked out by stones, trees etc. and upon which features such as burial mounds, temples and settlements grew. While the tracks themselves had long since vanished, these markers, or more modern replacements, could still be used to locate the original alignments. He christened these ancient tracks 'ley lines' or 'leys'. The word comes from the Old English '*lēah*', 'woodland' or 'woodland clearing', which gives rise to place-names such as Langley and Alderley (Watkins claims that the word had a prehistoric use, derived from the clearing of woodland to make way for a track). With great enthusiasm he developed his theories, and proceeded to find a vast number of ley lines across the country. His book *The Old*

Straight Track was published in 1925 and has remained in print almost ever since (Watkins 1994). Though Watkins' ideas were not, and have never been, accepted by professional archeologists or historians, amateur landscape enthusiasts soon took up his challenge, to go out and find ley lines for themselves. A Straight Track Club was soon formed, and a currently available magazine *The Ley Hunter* demonstrates that the subject is still popular. Yet the intervening years have seen Watkins' original ideas subsumed in a whole range of studies, by authors such as Alexander Thorn, John Michell and Paul Devereux, whose ideas range from the supposed ability of the builders of prehistoric stone circles to produce precise long-distance alignments, using landscape features and heavenly bodies, to wilder notions, such as the suggestion that ley lines are based on electro-magnetic lines of force, perhaps even used by UFOs as tracking guides! The most recent development is based on the theory that spirits of the dead travel in straight lines, and that it was awareness of this which led the ancients to construct straight tracks in the first place. A recent book by Danny Sullivan (Sullivan 1999), though written by an enthusiast, gives a balanced summary of the history of ley lines.

But reading such accounts, even balanced ones, can lend an air of plausibility to a theory which is based on no more than random pattern-making. Tom Williamson and Liz Bellamy (1983) have cast a sceptical eye over the original theory and found no substance to it at all. Apart from the implausibility of features of vastly different age being linked in some direct way, they show how easy it is, using a random process, to find a whole series of different straight alignments linking the same landscape features. Thus, ley lines can be seen as no more than imaginary constructs, along with the ancient civilisation which is supposed to have produced them. However, once released, this idea has run and run, and seems likely to continue to do so. It is to be hoped that this book demonstrates that, even if we confine ourselves to more credible evidence, the story of our road history is every bit as intriguing as the one conjured up by Alfred Watkins and his followers.

3

ROMAN ROADS TO MOTOR ROADS: OUR MODERN NETWORK EMERGES

INTRODUCTION

This chapter looks at where roads go, and the influences which determined, and continue to determine, their course through the landscape. Britain is covered with a dense mass of roads of all descriptions, which are available for public use; they are linked together in a series of nodes, which are more usually referred to as intersections or junctions (we shall use the last of these terms throughout this book). The totality of roads and junctions is usually described as a network, within which there may be sub-divisions, such as the national motorway network, the network of lanes round a village etc. The concept of a network is useful, but it may be misleading, because it gives the impression that it arises from a coherent planning process, whereas in practice almost all road networks have evolved gradually, being added to and altered over time to meet the ever-changing needs and demands of travellers. It is not even true to say that a particular class or category of roads came about in a coherent way; even our most recently built network of roads, the motorways designated for the exclusive use of motor vehicles, has been the result of nearly a century of thinking and rethinking about what should be built. What we see around us, then, is the result of centuries, even millennia of development, each new stage being tacked on to what was there already, with roads gaining and losing importance and sometimes being abandoned altogether in favour of something which seems to be more appropriate. It is this gradual process of development which we are concerned with in this chapter, as we trace how roads came to be where we see them.

ROMAN ROADS: BRITAIN'S FIRST STRATEGIC NETWORK

Of all the ancient tracks in Britain, it is the network built by the Romans which has attracted most study, and about which most is known (Margary 1973; Bagshawe 1994; Davies 2002). Ivan Margary traced about 6000 miles (10,000km) of this network (*12*). Many of these roads have been known as Roman routes for centuries, with antiquarians like Camden, Stukeley and Leland being able to follow sections of roads like Foss Way and Watling Street. Though there are sometimes local traditions and place-names which give a clue, the main reason that Roman roads can be identified is that they were constructed in a reasonably consistent way, using stone metalling, drainage ditches and an *agger*, a raised embankment upon which the road itself rests. While the metalling itself can easily be dispersed, and ditches filled in, by neglect or ploughing, or the whole structure can be buried by wind- or water-borne soil, the *agger* often remains visible, even if lower than it was originally. The fact that Roman routes are often quite straight and direct also helps to identify them in the modern landscape. We shall return to the Romans' construction methods in the next chapter; in this section we look briefly at where the roads went and how the network was built up.

When the Romans finally decided to invade these islands in AD 43 – Julius Caesar's two incursions nearly a century earlier did not constitute invasion – they would have known that most of the area was inhabited by tribes who controlled local areas, with most people living in small settlements or isolated farms. Overland transport links comprised unmade tracks linking the places where people lived to their fields, pastures or woodland, or to neighbouring settlements. Longer journeys would be made by travelling along a series of these local links. It seems clear that the Romans did not consider these existing tracks as adequate. While they may have been suitable for an essentially local, tribal economy, the Romans needed a system of roads which would allow their army and administration to operate across the whole area. So, almost as soon as the legions landed, their engineers started to prepare the extensive network that we can observe today.

This network, the principal elements of which are shown in figure *12*, contains several routes, such as Watling Street, Foss Way, Devil's Highway and Dere Street, that seem to suggest planning and design on a strategic scale, with places over

ROMAN ROADS TO MOTOR ROADS: OUR MODERN NETWORK EMERGES

12 Principal Roman roads

50 miles (80km) apart, such as London and Chichester, being linked by fairly direct routes. Whether there was ever a strategic plan of where roads should go, perhaps marked on a map, is not known. We can surmise that accurate surveying techniques would have been needed to determine such long routes, but decisions would still have been needed to determine which places were to be served. A glance at the map shows that fortresses, such as Lincoln, York, Wroxeter, Chester and Caerleon were well served by roads; as were important tribal centres such as Silchester, Cirencester and Leicester, along with ports such as Dover, Ravenglass and Newcastle.

Viewing a map such as that in figure *12*, with its well-established routes of famous roads, can give the impression of an impressive, but essentially static

41

system, built soon after the Roman army arrived in AD 43 and remaining in place until they left, nearly four centuries later. Reality is very different; the first roads were quite modest, both in their construction and length, and it probably took nearly a century to complete the main routes across the whole area. Even while new roads were being built, existing ones were being repaired, widened or made narrower, or even abandoned altogether.

Unfortunately, while we can often identify these activities from excavation, it is seldom possible to put an accurate date to either the building or subsequent repair of a particular road. We can assume that, to begin with, the network developed to support the Roman army's campaign. As the army moved forward, lightly built roads would have been constructed behind, to provide a link to their nearest base. These early routes would not have looked particularly impressive by the standards of what we think a Roman road should be like; perhaps comprising just a cleared strip of land, with rudimentary drainage and metalling (Peddie 1997, 188). It might have been many years before proper drainage ditches were dug, the famous *agger* formed from the material from these ditches, and layers of metalling laid on top. Because of the difficulty of putting precise dates on the building of particular roads, it is not possible to be sure which came first. However, enough is known about the progress of the invasion to make a guess at how the network was built up (*13*). There would have been two categories of road; penetration roads gave a direct link between the army in the field and its base, while territory-holding roads were built laterally, to ensure that Roman influence would reach across an area being occupied (Davies 2002, 116) (*13*).

It seems fairly clear that the first road linked the invasion beach-head at Richborough to a Thames crossing at Southwark, and from there carried through to the first legionary base at Colchester. As soon as this base was established, roads would probably have been built to the main Iron Age tribal settlements at Leicester, St Albans, Silchester and Caistor. Over the next 40 years, as the army moved west and north, the roads followed, across what is now England, into Wales and up to Scotland.

While London may have grown to dominate the road network, other places became important centres too. Towns such as Gloucester, Lincoln, York and Chester benefited, as did London, from both road and river access. Silchester, on the other hand, had no river access at all, yet, if its position in the road network is anything to go by, became an important centre of traffic and communication (*14*).

Another town, Wroxeter, began life as a legionary fortress, but continued as an important centre even when the army moved up to Chester, because it lay on the road which ran up the Welsh Marches from the fortress at Caerleon.

The two roads flanking the Pennines seem to have remained of primarily military value, as vital links with Hadrian's Wall and the Antonine Wall. Their repair

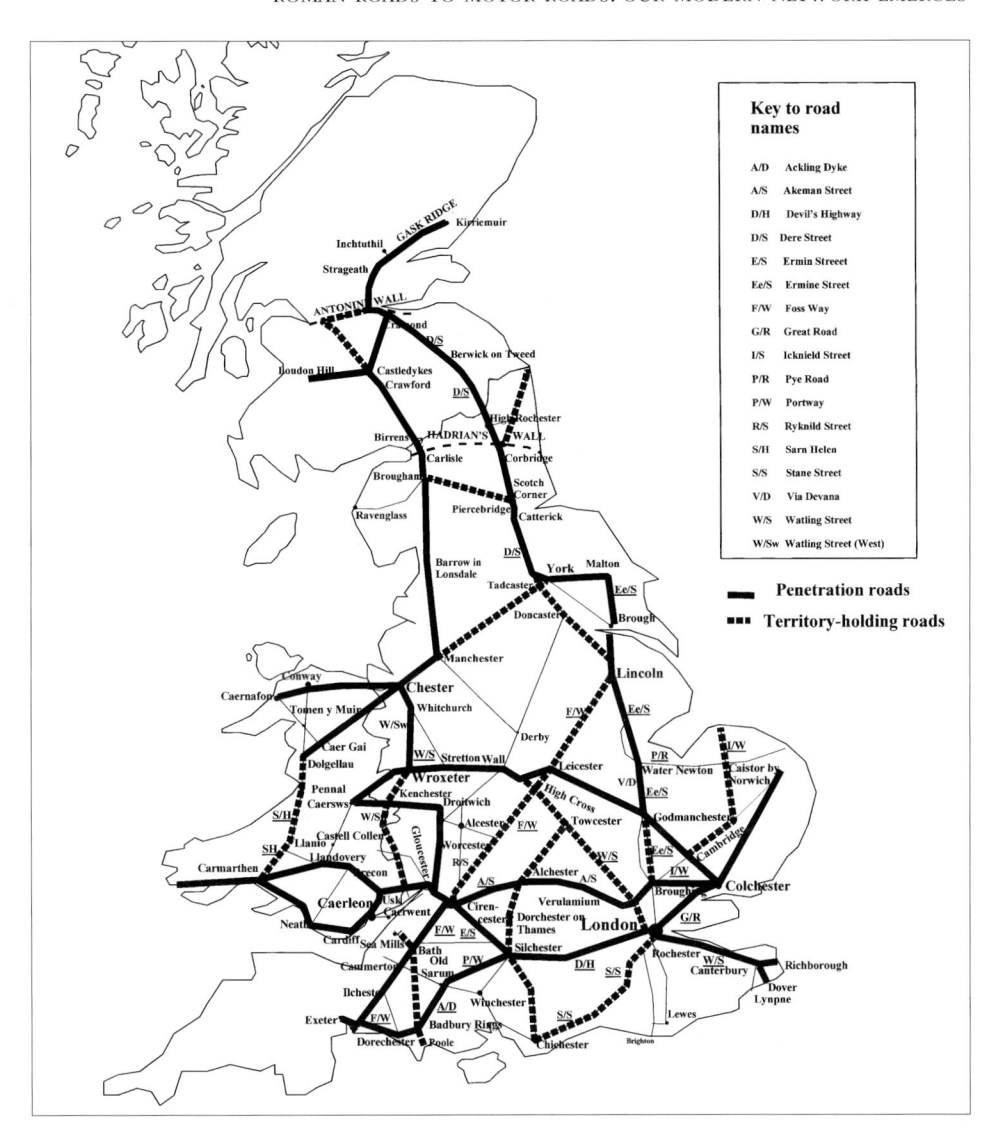

13 Suggested course of the first roads built by the Romans after their invasion in AD 43

and re-repair can, to a certain extent, be linked to the changing policy concerning the occupation of Northern England and Scotland. The most northerly road, running up the Gask Ridge from the Antonine Wall, was exclusively military, being abandoned when the forts along it were abandoned, as the army eventually pulled back to Hadrian's Wall in the second century (*15, 16*).

Efforts were made to maintain those roads which were still important for either military or civilian traffic; this demonstrates that, in a society where urban life was an important element, roads were indispensable to maintain the

14 Reconstruction drawing of a street in Roman Silchester. *Margaret Matthews*

15 The line of the most northerly Roman road, along the Gask Ridge, west of Perth, where a minor modern road follows the Roman line; the photograph shows a point where the modern road veers away (to the left) to cross a bridge at Trinity Gask, before returning to the Roman line further on

ROMAN ROADS TO MOTOR ROADS: OUR MODERN NETWORK EMERGES

16 Roman Dere Street, near Jedburgh on the English/Scottish border. A minor modern road and droveway follow the Roman line

economy. We next look at what happened when the Roman army was recalled in the early fifth century.

THE ANGLO-SAXON PERIOD

The three or four centuries following the withdrawal of the Roman legions saw a complex interaction between the Romano-British (those who inhabited these islands during the Roman period) and newcomers (Angles, Saxons, Danes and Norwegians). Controversy still rages as to the extent of population movement, but it seems clear that the Roman-style urban economy quickly collapsed. Even if people continued to live within the walls of the old Roman towns, they did so as squatters, with no attempt to function as an urban community. As a consequence there was no need for a Roman-type, high-quality road system to serve the towns and provide strategic links across the islands. Yet, so well built were these roads, that they continued to serve a useful purpose, both as transport links and land boundaries.

And in one important respect, we owe a debt to this period, for, during it, the famous and familiar names which we use to identify Roman roads began to appear.

The main source of evidence for this naming process are the Anglo-Saxon land charters, used by people to establish and enforce their claim to a particular parcel of land. In order to identify the boundaries of the claim, a charter contained descriptions of features in the landscape: streams, hills, prominent trees, paths etc. Occasionally, one of the boundaries is identified as, for example, *Earminga stræt* or *Wæclinga stræt* (Cameron 1996, 156). These are Old English terms which are usually interpreted, respectively, as 'well-built road of the Earmingas (Earn's people)' and 'well-built road of the Wæclingas (Wacol's people)'. While it is not difficult to see how these names could evolve into our present day 'Ermine Street' and 'Watling Street', studying the process by which this occurred can tell us something about the Anglo-Saxon use of, and attitude to, the roads left from the Roman era.

Careful study of charter boundary descriptions by scholars has enabled the term *stræt* or *stræte* to be associated with Roman roads. It is not clear that the Anglo-Saxons thought of them as having been built by the Romans, though they almost certainly recognised them as of ancient origin, but it has enabled us to be able to associate the word 'street' with what we now know are roads of Roman origin, while place-names such as Streatley and Stratford lie on their course. Though we do not know who exactly Earn's or Wacol's people were, the location of the charters suggests that they inhabited areas near Cambridge and St Albans respectively; thus the charter writers were probably referring to an essentially local name for the roads concerned. Only gradually did these names come to be associated with significant lengths of Roman road, running from London to the Humber in the case of Ermin Street, and from the Kent coast, through London, to Wroxeter in the case of Watling Street. We can follow the same process for the several dozen other names which have become associated with Roman roads. As time passed, an essentially local name seems to have spread along the road, giving us a convenient way of identifying a route, and lending a certain air of romance to each such road. But it is important to recognise that the process was arbitrary and far from clear-cut. For example, besides Ermine Street running north from London, there is Ermine Street from Silchester to Gloucester via Cirencester; again, there are several Watling Streets, besides the main one from Kent to Wroxeter, including the road down through the Welsh Marches, now known as Watling Street (West). Other roads have a confusing mixture of similar names and spellings such as Ryknield (or Ryknild) Street, Icknield (or Icknild) Street, while there are several Stone and Stane Streets. So when we use these names today, we should be aware that, often, it is no more than a convention, and certainly tells us nothing about the Roman names, or even whether the Romans would have agreed about which lengths of a particular road should be identified with a single name.

Traditional Roman road names are not exclusively Old English in origin. For example, Stanegate, south of Hadrian's Wall, employs the Old Norse word *gata* meaning 'road'. Latin seems to influence the naming of Foss (or Fosse) Way (both spellings appear in land charters), derived from *fossa* for a ditch or bank.

The Celtic language tradition is evident in Wales, where Roman roads are often associated with the word *Sarn* (causeway). We saw in Chapter 2 that two roads carry the name Sarn Helen, but there are others, though not themselves carrying traditional names, which nevertheless pass through or close to places called Sarn, such as the two in Powys and one near Bridgend. In this sense Sarn may play the same role as Street (or Strat-) in England, though, as it is based on the Celtic language, it can probably claim an older association with Roman roads than its Anglo-Saxon equivalent.

It seems reasonable to conclude that the roads inherited from the Roman period were made use of during the centuries that followed it. Though names in the charters, such as *heah stræt* (High Street), *Bradan stræt* (Broad Street), *Saltstræt* (Salt Street) etc. usually seem to be associated with known Roman roads, other terms for roads appear, such as *weg*, *pa* and *lane*, which give rise to modern 'way', 'path' and 'lane'. Della Hooke has studied the charters in the West Midlands area to produce the likely course of Anglo-Saxon roads and tracks (Hooke 1981). Many other scholars have contributed to a collection of county-based studies, edited by Jeremy Haslam, which show the likely course of Anglo-Saxon routes in Southern England (Haslam 1984).

Thus we may conclude that there was a complex network of roads, tracks and pathways, well adapted to the requirements of the time; traffic was probably not intensive, with pack animals and pedestrians predominating. Many of these routes were not metalled, so are difficult to trace physically; we know of them through the documentary evidence of the charters. But it is clear that the process of adapting the Roman inheritance for later requirements began very quickly; the next section shows how we can begin to use map evidence from the Norman and late medieval periods to show how our modern network had begun to emerge.

ROMAN TO MEDIEVAL: THE MODERN NETWORK EMERGES

Introduction
As we saw in the previous section there were many local tracks in use after Britain ceased to be part of the Roman Empire. Yet it seems clear that for many

journeys, long and short, the Roman road system remained in use. While it is reasonable to assume that the Roman road network still did good service, a process was soon underway which would necessitate some major new links. This process was the growth of towns, a process which got under way in the ninth century; these generated traffic, which in turn demanded roads. Where the towns were based on what had been Roman towns, like Chester, the existing Roman road network could provide good access. But many post-Roman towns, like Marlborough, lay away from Roman roads, with the result that new tracks and roads grew up to serve them. A new system of roads evolved, part Roman, part medieval, a system which forms the basis of our modern network (other than the twentieth-century motorways). One way of charting this process would be to study maps showing the road network at different stages. As we have seen, archaeology and historical sources have enabled us to build up a good picture of the Roman road network, but it is over 1000 years from the end of the Roman period before reasonably detailed road maps begin to be published, such as John Ogilby's *Britannia* (Ogilby 1675). We have already seen that Matthew Paris produced two maps of Britain, showing the Four Royal Roads and an itinerary from Newcastle to Dover. However, neither map provides sufficient detail for our purpose. Fortunately, there is one other medieval example, known as the Gough Map, which can enable us to see the modern road network as it begins to break away from the Roman inheritance.

The Gough Map

The map is held in the Bodleian Library in Oxford, from whom a facsimile edition can be obtained. A detailed description and annotation is provided by E.J.S. Parsons and Sir Frank Stenton (Parsons and Stenton 1958). By using the style of lettering as a guide it is reasonably certain that the map dates to about 1350, though it is not possible to trace its provenance back that far. It is named after Richard Gough, an antiquarian who had inherited and studied the map, before bequeathing it to the Bodleian Library in 1809. The trail can be traced back to the seventeenth century, but no further. So the map's originator is not known, neither is its precise purpose; for example was it intended for general use by travellers, or was it made to help a particular institution, such as the church, in the conduct of its affairs? This uncertainty should make us cautious about reading too much into the map, but nevertheless it has proved an invaluable source of information.

The map contains the names and locations of many towns and the course of the main rivers. From the point of view of the present work however, it is the existence of a number of road links between towns, shown as straight lines, which are of most interest. It is reasonable to associate these with usable roads;

17 Map showing primary and secondary routes which appear on the Gough Map, c.AD 1350, superimposed on the map of Roman roads (12)

these can be linked together into a series, which suggests the concept of through routes or journeys (*17*).

The map above shows these routes, superimposed on the map of Roman roads (*12*). Those locations which are not included on the Gough Map are retained for information, but reduced in size and printed in regular type. Locations which are common to the two maps are shown in bold type, along with a selection of towns which are on the Gough Map, but, having no Roman origin, do not appear on a map of Roman roads. The primary Gough routes are shown as thick lines, with some of the secondary ones slightly narrower and the Roman roads are shown by the narrowest lines.

There are modern routes along all the Gough routes, and, apart from some local modifications to increase width, straighten bends and ease gradients (see Chapter 5), these follow almost the same course as their medieval predecessors. Thus, by comparing the course of these roads with earlier, Roman, roads in the same area, we can see what changes have occurred, and in some cases, find reasons why.

Most of the principal routes radiate from London, much as roads do today, and indeed have done since Roman London became dominant in the late first century. Two of these follow closely the Roman line for some distance; going north, Roman Ermine Street is followed by the Great North Road, though the latter veers away at the approach to the Roman town of Water Newton, to head through Wansford and Stamford (*18*), then north-west across the country, eventually joining with the west coast route to Carlisle at Kendal.

Heading north-west from London, Roman Watling Street is followed as far as Wall. Here the Gough route heads for Chester and thence to Carlisle, while the Roman version of Watling Street turned west to reach the important Roman town of Wroxeter; this did not reappear after it was abandoned. The busy Roman road linking Caerleon, Wroxeter and Chester is represented today by a minor track through the Roman remains at Wroxeter.

Running west from London, the Roman road to Silchester is replaced by three Gough routes, which closely follow the modern network. The Roman crossing of the Thames at Staines is replaced by bridges at Kingston and Maidenhead, while the third route, to Oxford and Gloucester, keeps to the north side of the Thames valley. Silchester, like Wroxeter, was never re-occupied after the Roman period, and now lies at the centre of a maze of narrow lanes, none of which coincide with the important Roman roads to the town.

Along the west coast of Wales and Northern England, there are Gough and Roman routes running parallel, but with very different characteristics. Both routes were important military connections in the Roman period, and took a fairly direct course, some distance inland. By contrast, the Gough routes, closely followed by their modern equivalents, keep further west, and often make diversions to reach coastal towns (*19*).

Another realignment is evident on the road running due west from London. The Roman road, having reached Silchester, branches off the road to Cirencester, and makes a direct line to just north of Bath. The medieval route passed through Reading (the town which grew up in place of Roman Silchester), and makes diversions to pass through or near to Marlborough, Avebury and Chippenham. The modern A4, though somewhat straighter than its medieval forebear, is still not as direct as the original Roman line.

The Gough Map has limitations. It is clear that the coverage of Britain is uneven; there are missing sections which should have been known to the

18 Bridge over the river Welland at Stamford, Lincolnshire. The town has Anglo-Saxon origins as an important staging point on the Great North Road

map-maker. There are no routes in Scotland, none up the east side of Northern England, and none running from London to Kent and Sussex. Another missing section is the road which runs from Swindon, up through Cirencester to

19 The A6 at Shap Fell, looking north. The steep ascent requires a zig-zag course to alleviate the gradient. The equivalent Roman road is about a mile (1.6km) inland, to the east, though the separation is greater further south

Gloucester. This is the Roman Ermin Street, which is closely followed by the A419 and A417, and thus seems to have been in almost continuous use for nearly 2000 years.

However, the roads which are shown provide a valuable guide to what had happened by the time the map was produced. Though those routes which are shown no doubt grew up gradually, by the mid-fourteenth century, the process of adapting the Roman network to medieval needs had largely been completed. Though some Roman routes remained, and still remain, in use, many others have been bypassed or superceded. Even well-made and direct roads will not survive if they do not match changing requirements. Medieval settlement patterns often changed from Roman ones, and the road network needed to change too.

TURNPIKES

Introduction
With the end of the medieval era in 1485, there followed a period of comparative stability. Economic growth had the effect of increasing traffic demand, with consequent greater wear on the roads. While central government had taken an interest in bridge-building from the Norman period onwards, most statutes sought to lay responsibility on local landowners, religious houses or local boroughs to construct and maintain them. Roads received less attention, but an Act of 1556 set up an arrangement whereby each parish had to elect people, who, in conjunction with Church Wardens, had the duty of requiring all citizens to provide labour and/or materials for work on the roads in their area (2 and 3 Philip and Mary c. 8, see Appendix). Subsequent measures tinkered with this system, increasing the number of days required, and requiring that someone had to be appointed as surveyor. While towns had some resources to cope with their own roads, rural parishes, through which main roads lay, found the burden intolerable, and began to petition Parliament for some redress. Most vociferous were parishes along the Old and New Great North Roads (the former going through Royston along the Roman Ermine Street and now A10 and A1198, the latter through Biggleswade along modern A1). The parishioners of Standon in Hertfordshire pointed out in one such petition, in 1656, that there would be insufficient funds to maintain their 2-mile (3.2km) section of the Old Great North Road, even if the whole income of the parish was devoted to the task (Webb and Webb 1920, 114). Although proposals were made for some central funding and supervision of road-building and maintenance, these always failed on the grounds that they represented further taxation. Eventually it was the proposal for the setting up of a local trust, covering a specific length of road and financed by tolls, which was successful; in 1663 the first Turnpike Act was passed (15 Charles II c. 1). In the preamble it is stated that heavy wagon traffic was coming from East Anglia and heading for Ware, for transfer to boats for the journey

to London. To finance the repairs which were necessary to keep up with this traffic, toll gates were to be set up at Wadesmill, Caxton and Stilton, between Ware and Huntingdon. In the event it seems that only the Wadesmill toll was retained, and it was some time before other trusts came into existence, but nevertheless a precedent had been set. Between 1663 and 1800 there were over 700 new Trust Acts, with 31 being passed in the peak year of 1765 (Pawson 1977, Appendix 1).

By 1750 many main streets in London had become Turnpike Trusts, and, as can be seen from the figure, the radial routes out of the capital had begun to spread across the country, though not necessarily as far as the coast (*20*). Though Edinburgh could be reached, there were still gaps in the Great North Road and the east coast route in Scotland. Despite a heavy concentration of roads in the Welsh Marches, turnpikes had not extended into Wales itself. Much of the impetus for the setting up of turnpikes was to take advantage of tolls from industrial traffic, such as coal and iron ore; it was the development of coalmining in Wales over the next few decades which saw a rapid expansion westwards (Pawson 1977, 153).

As we have seen, the basis of our road network had formed centuries earlier; turnpikes usually comprised either rebuilding of existing roads or a new, fairly local, diversion (*21*).

Though there have been question marks over both the financial and technical competence of the trusts, they did undoubtedly make significant improvements. A measure of this can be obtained from the reduction in travel time to London from our major cities (*22*). Average speeds which were not much above walking pace in the 1600s had increased to about 10mph by the mid-1800s. Improved roads must have played a major part, though for long journeys, at least, other factors were important, such as the ability to travel overnight, and to change horses at regular intervals (*23, 24*).

Though there were undoubted improvements to the network as a result of the Turnpike Acts, the problem of financing and implementing road-building and maintenance was far from solved. Tolls were unpopular, leading to many riots and the destruction of toll gates or bars (Albert 1979). Also trusts themselves were often inefficient and even corrupt, with their income seldom being sufficient to keep their roads in good repair while giving a return to investors. Gradually these roads were taken over by local government authorities, with finance coming from general taxation. During the nineteenth century the capacity of local government to run public services had improved, initially with the Victorian drive to improve sanitation (Smith 2004, 20). A body called the Local Government Board oversaw these activities, and, with the passing of the 1872 Public Health Act, the board gradually took over responsibility for roads formerly controlled by Turnpike

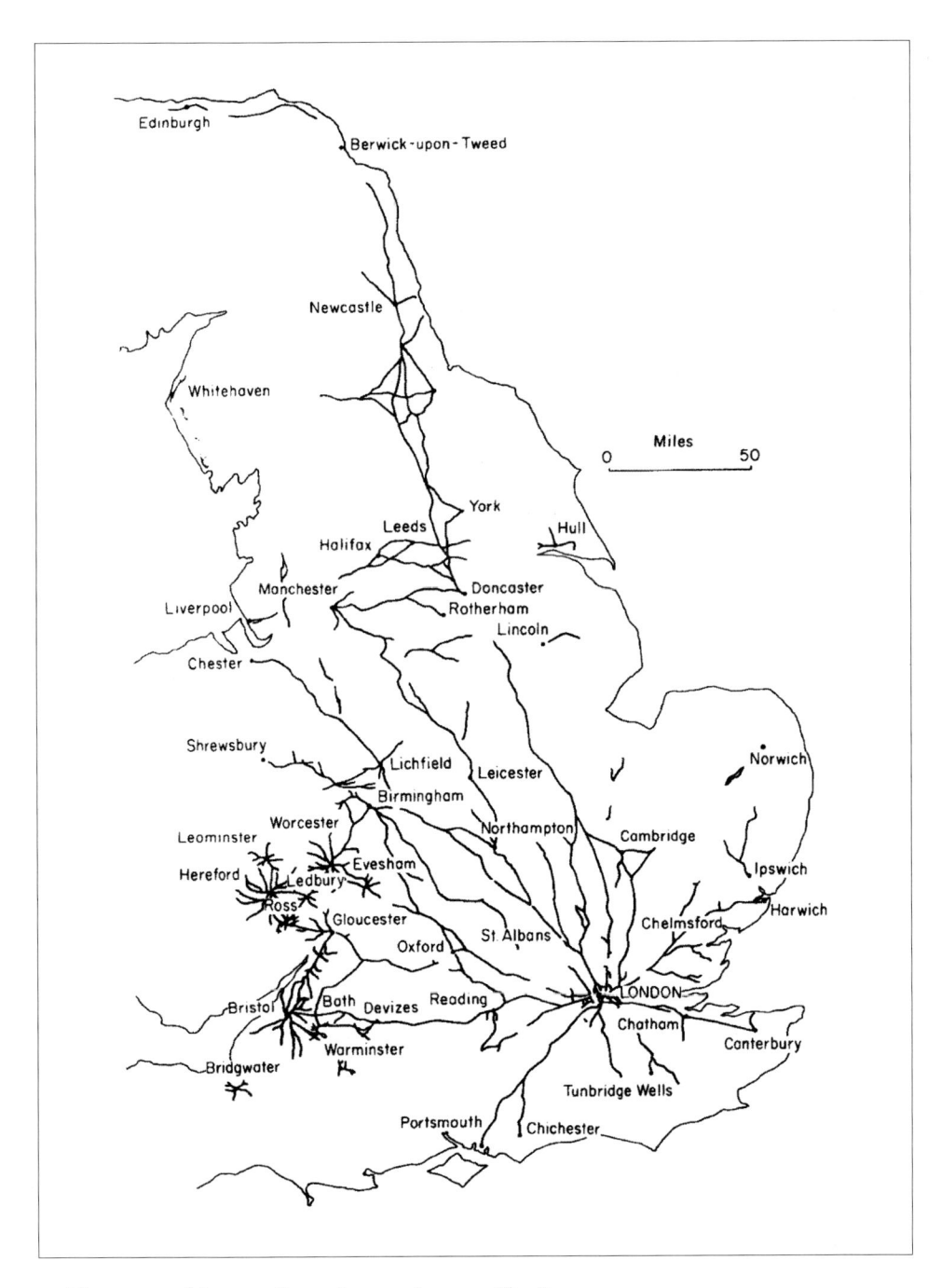

20 The extent of the turnpike road system in 1750. *After Pawson 1977, 140*

21 Present-day footpath following the course of a short-lived, eighteenth-century diversion to avoid the steep gradient of Watling Street at Puddlehill, Hertfordshire

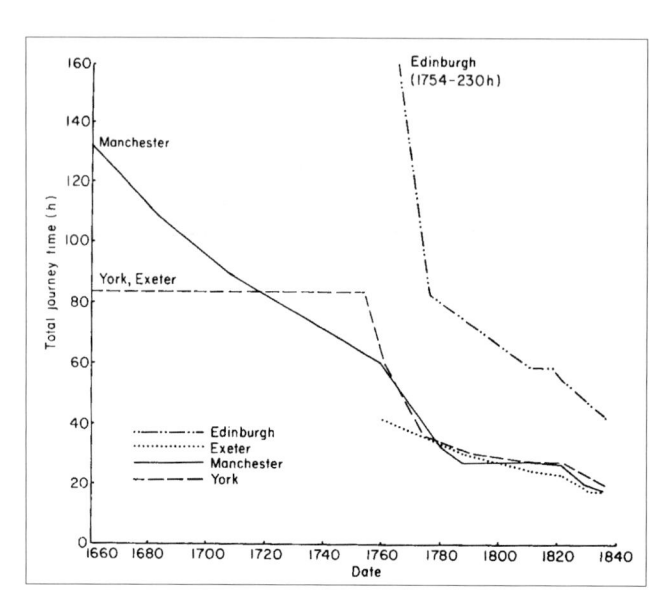

22 Changes in travel times by stage-coach between London and four major cities, between 1660 and 1840. After Pawson 1977, figure 40

ROMAN ROADS TO MOTOR ROADS: OUR MODERN NETWORK EMERGES

23 High Street, Abington, Lanarkshire, in about 1912, with the Abington Hotel, opened in 1896, to the left. The hotel and its predecessor gave accommodation to stage-coach travellers on the main road, from Carlisle to Glasgow. Ahead, at the fork, Glasgow lay to the left, Edinburgh to the right. The road still carries a 'macadamised' surface (see Chapter 4). *Courtesy Biggar Museum*

24 Recent view of High Street, Abington, Lanarkshire, with the Abington Hotel, to the left. Only the right fork now carries through traffic because both village and hotel have been bypassed twice, first by the A74 in the 1960s, and again in the 1990s by the M74

Trusts. Thus, the two-centuries-long experiment of privatising Britain's principal roads, came to an end.

THE ENCLOSURE MOVEMENT

Towards the end of the medieval period and in the two centuries which followed, a slow process had been taking place, by which previously open field systems and common land began to be enclosed. The countryside was thus gradually being parcelled up, each enclosed area belonging to a single landowner. Hedges or walls were established to mark out the boundaries, and our familiar patchwork of fields began to emerge. Probably the effect on the road system was not great, as the new boundaries often respected old but well-established roads and tracks. Some of these were the major routes we have been looking at, while others were much more local, having grown up haphazardly over a long period. However, in the eighteenth century, the pattern changed dramatically. Landowners and other prominent local people began to sponsor parliamentary bills to 'enclose' land in a specified area, usually a parish. A surveyor was appointed to produce a plan of where the new boundaries were to be placed and where the roads between would go. Thus a formal system began to replace the earlier, informal one, though the latter did not entirely disappear (Kain, Chapman and Oliver 2004, 9). Most of these new layouts were very regular, but because of the way the surveyors

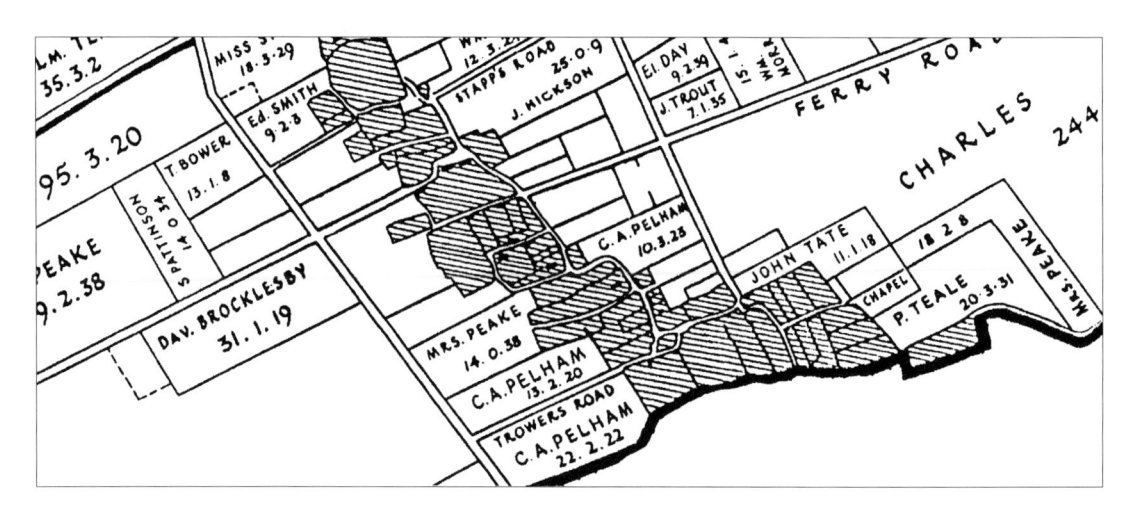

25 An enclosure map of North and South Killingholme, Lincolnshire. In 1777-8 the area was enclosed under parliamentary control (unshaded), leaving part (shaded) subject to the older, informal system. Note the abrupt changes in the width, direction and straightness of roads as they cross the boundary. *Rex Russell*

designed the new roads, and the way they interacted with neighbouring areas which may have already been enclosed in a less regular way (Hindle 2001, 119), road width, direction and straightness could all change abruptly at the boundaries between these enclosed areas (*25*).

CENTRAL GOVERNMENT'S FIRST ROAD PROJECTS

Introduction

During the whole of the early medieval, medieval and early modern periods, building and maintaining roads and bridges was an essentially local responsibility. Even the coming of turnpikes in the seventeenth and eighteenth centuries did not alter the position. True, the Turnpike Trusts offered a new way of financing roads, via tolls, and the setting up of a trust could only occur with Parliament's specific authority, but once set up, the operation and financing of turnpikes was entirely independent of government. But there were three exceptions to this rule, when, for essentially political reasons, central government found itself directly involved in road-building; these projects were the building of the military roads in the Highlands of Scotland (Wade's Roads), their later replacement with a civil network, and the upgrading of the London to Holyhead Road, both of which were the responsibility of Thomas Telford.

The military roads in the Scottish Highlands (Wade's Roads)

People seldom welcome influences imposed from outside their area. Perhaps because of the terrain, the inhabitants of the Scottish Highlands have resisted such influence more fiercely than most. The Roman Empire never encompassed the area, and even the succession of James VI of Scotland to the English throne in 1603, and the Act of Union just over a century later did not mean the area was integrated with the rest of Britain. Despite frequent uprisings, the government in London preferred to work through local aristocratic allies rather than attempt a permanent presence. All this was to change when one such ally, Simon Fraser, Lord Lovat, wrote to the king in 1724 to point out how dangerous the situation was in the Highlands. Though his motives have been questioned, the result was, in hindsight at any rate, quite dramatic. The government appointed Major-General George Wade, Member of Parliament for Bath, to travel to the area and report back. His report was mainly about the repair or establishment of forts, the disarming of irregular clan forces, the better organisation of locally recruited soldiers and their coordination with central government units. There was only a brief mention of the need for better roads, but after his appointment in 1728 as Commander-in-Chief, North Britain, he put in hand a programme of road and

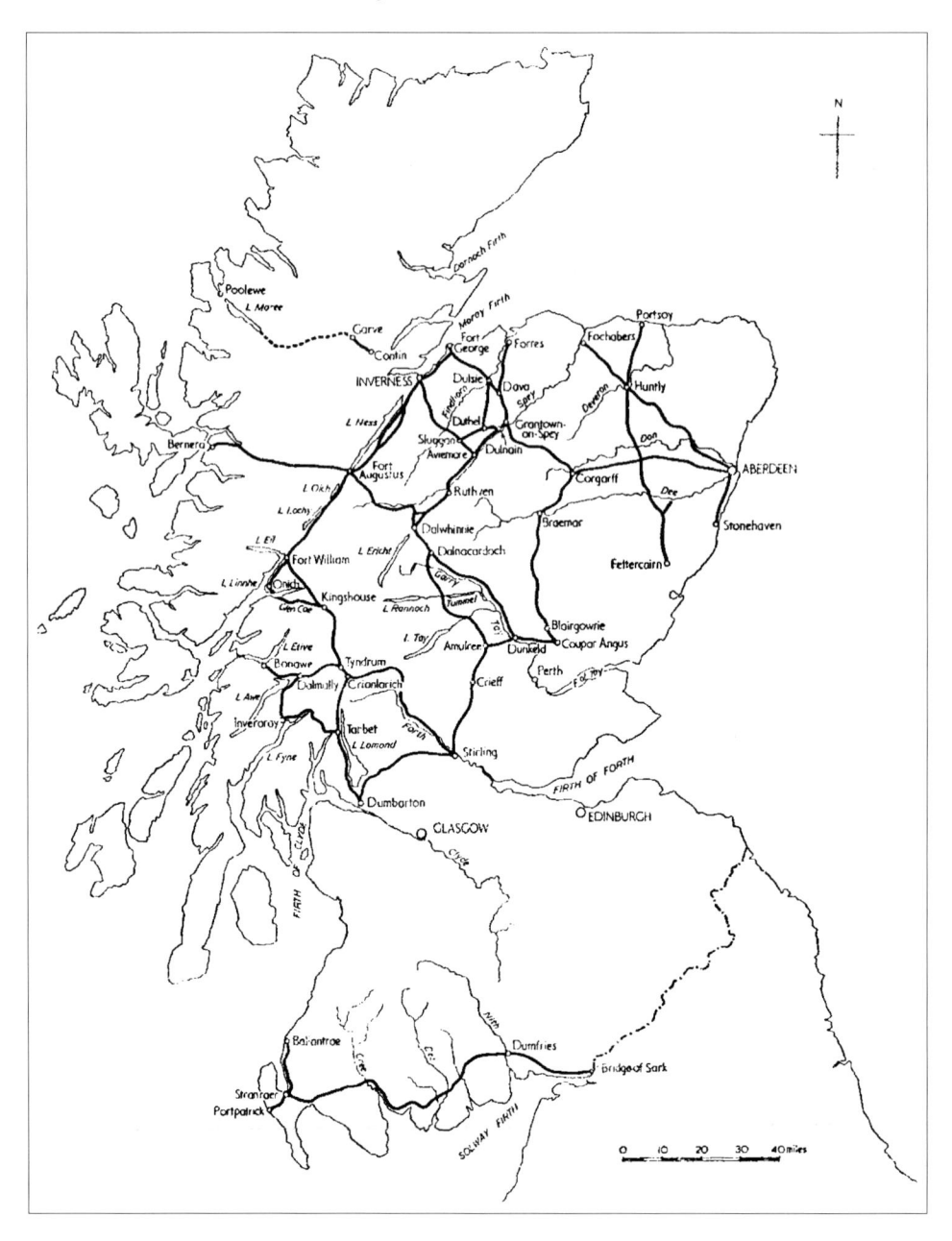

26 Map showing the extent of the military road network, built in the eighteenth century to counter Jacobite resistance in the Scottish Highlands. After Taylor 1996, 9

bridge-building; despite the fact that the programme continued long after his recall for other duties in 1740, and that many of these roads are no longer in use, his name has become almost synonymous with roads in the Highlands.

The progress of this work is described by William Taylor (1996) (*26*). Wade's first priority was to link the forts at Fort William, Fort Augustus and Inverness by building a road up the Great Glen. He also had a small boat built for ferrying men and supplies on Loch Ness. He clearly took a critical view of his work; dissatisfied with the alignment of his original Great Glen Road along Loch Ness – it had been built in a fairly direct line with little concern for gradient – he had it realigned nearer to the loch side, necessitating much excavation and dynamiting. In all he built about 250 miles (380km) of road, mainly concentrating on the north–south communication which was needed to support his troop deployments. It seems likely that, had it not been for the '45 rebellion, military road-building in the Highlands might have come to a halt with Wade's departure in 1740. However, panic caused by that event ensured that the work continued for most of the eighteenth century; eventually over 1000 miles (1600km) of military roads were constructed. Thus, Wade's contribution was only a quarter of the total, but so strong was his influence that the whole network tends to carry his name. However, he had left the road programme in the capable hands of William Caulfeild, who could thus make an equal claim of influence, but whose name, by comparison with Wade's, is largely forgotten.

The '45 rebellion gave greater impetus to an important and difficult cross route from Stirling to Fort William. Though it was completed in 1753, only seven years later the northern section was completely changed to avoid the very steep ground near the northern end. Instead of the direct route from Fort William to Kinghouse via Kinlochleven and the Devil's Staircase, a longer but easier diversion was made, through Onich, over a ferry at Balaculish and thence through Glencoe (*27, 28, 29, 30, 31*).

As the eighteenth century drew to a close, the growing fashion for rapid civilian travel in wheeled vehicles began to show that military roads were still too steep and precipitous. With the arrival of Thomas Telford in 1801, a process of replacement and realignment was begun, so that for today's travellers in the Scottish Highlands, it is the work of Telford, rather than Wade and Caulfeild, which is likely to form the basis of their routes (Rolt 1985, 74ff).

The Holyhead Road

The Act of Union between Britain and Ireland, in 1801, focused attention on the poor state of communication between London and Dublin. The first problem seemed to be that there were no proper harbours on either side of the Irish Sea; accordingly, John Rennie and Joseph Huddard were appointed to examine the situation. They recommended Holyhead, on the north-west coast of Anglesey, and Howth, and, after several years' delay, they were contracted to

27 The Devil's Staircase, a steep section of the eighteenth-century military road network near Glencoe, Highland Region. Now a popular track for walkers, it joins the modern road (A82) to the right of the clump of trees (centre-right)

put the necessary works in hand. No mention was made of roads; indeed Rennie is reputed to have believed that road-making was beneath the notice of civil engineers (Rolt 1985, 124).

This view notwithstanding, there was certainly something very wrong with road access to Anglesey, and across it. The route from London to Shrewsbury was in the hands of 15 Turnpike Trusts; though the road was passable, allowing mail coaches to reach Shrewsbury, it was mostly in poor condition. Between Shrewsbury and Holyhead there were seven more trusts, but their inadequacy was such that mail coaches could not move beyond Shrewsbury, and even the riding post frequently lost horses because of injury.

That central government was persuaded to finance and organise the improvement of the Holyhead Road was the achievement of Sir Henry Parnell, the Member of Parliament for Queen's County in Ireland. He not only successfully lobbied for the setting up of the Holyhead Road Commission in 1815, but chaired it, and took an active and detailed interest in the work and in

28 The Devil's Staircase, Glencoe, Highland Region, part of the eighteenth-century military road network. In the foreground, a stream crosses the track via an open drainage channel, to protect the stone metalling from being washed away

29 Balaculish Bridge, over Loch Leven, looking west. The bridge was built in the 1960s to replace a ferry, the northern terminal of which can be seen in the foreground

the emerging science of road-building. For the next 36 years the government paid directly, first for major improvements to the road and then for upkeep and maintenance.

The road was a triumph of heavy engineering; hugely expensive by the standard of the times but also hugely inspiring and overwhelmingly successful in achieving its objectives. Though Parnell's involvement, and continued government funding were important, the triumphant outcome must be put down to the skills of its engineer, Thomas Telford. He built the road as he built his canals and bridges, to last for centuries. Perhaps the most famous structure is the Menai Bridge. It was opened to the public in 1826, but the public had taken a close interest all through its construction, and when Telford arrived in Bangor in April 1825 to supervise the slinging of the first cable, huge crowds gathered to watch. This bridge remains a spectacular feature (*32*).

ROMAN ROADS TO MOTOR ROADS: OUR MODERN NETWORK EMERGES

30 View looking west from Balaculish bridge, towards the mouth of Loch Leven

31 Military road, west of Kinghouse, Highland Region, with modern A82 to the left

65

32 Thomas Telford's Menai Bridge, a vital link on the Holyhead Road

Yet his road-building, on the route from Shrewsbury to the bridge, and beyond across Anglesey, while equally spectacular, is easily missed because of its modern 'feel' for drivers. Telford built the road with a prevailing gradient which was at, or below, 1 in 20, with no sharp bends; this compares with the 1 in 9 gradients and many sharp bends which existing travellers had to contend with. Once provided with a modern bituminous surface, speeds of 50 or 60mph are easily attainable, on a road which was intended to allow horse-drawn coaches to travel safely at 10mph. Whereas the existing turnpike routes twisted and turned, climbed and fell as they threaded their way along valleys and over passes, Telford's roads were built in deep cuttings, high embankments, across bridges or on rock-cut terraces (*33, 34*).

There can be no higher tribute to Telford's achievement in pushing a high-quality road through such mountainous terrain than the fact that it remains a satisfactory and busy road today. Of course it was successful in his day too,

33 Telford's Holyhead Road, on a high terrace as it approaches Lake Ogwen, Conway. The photograph is taken from the line of an earlier turnpike road

though the coming of the railway to Holyhead, less than a quarter century after the road's completion, meant that its value as a strategic route for horse-drawn vehicles was short-lived. Telford foresaw the coming of motorised road vehicles, albeit steam powered, and hoped that a steam-carriage service could operate on the Holyhead Road (Rolt 1985, 170). However, the imposition of high tolls and speed limits for such vehicles meant that it was not until the twentieth century, with the coming of the internal combustion engine, that Telford's Holyhead Road achieved its full potential.

Yet this success brings problems of its own. It has been recognised recently that, good though Telford's road is, pressure to raise its capacity to meet increasing traffic demand can lead to the destruction of Telford's original fabric. A desire to conserve this fabric, along with the original character of the road, has led to a decision to avoid major road-works along it (Quartermain, Trinder and Turner 2003).

FROM TRACKWAYS TO MOTORWAYS: 5000 YEARS OF HIGHWAY HISTORY

34 A further view of the high terrace, by means of which Telford's Holyhead Road avoids steep gradients and sharp bends, as it passes through a deep valley west of Lake Ogwen, Conway

MOTOR ROADS AND MOTORWAYS

During the nineteenth century roads were still the province of horse-riders, horse-drawn vehicles and pedestrians, with the occasional steam-powered vehicle (the internal combustion engine had only just begun to appear in the 1890s – see Chapter 6). By the middle of the century, roads were probably in a better state than they had ever been, even counting the Roman roads. The rapid rise of the railways, offering cheaper and quicker travel for both freight and passengers, tended to relegate roads to local feeder status, serving railway stations and areas where there were no rail services to compete with. Thus the first motor vehicles inherited a somewhat neglected road system, with many poor surfaces and rather steep gradients (see Chapter 5). As the number of motor cars and lorries rose, overtaking that of horse-drawn vehicles in the early 1920s, a process began by which ordinary roads were converted to carry self-propelled vehicles, with pneumatic tyres, instead of horse-drawn ones with solid wheels. As we shall see in the next chapter, the great success of the macadamised roads, with their tightly packed structure of small stones, proved inadequate for rubber-tyred wheels; instead of compacting the surface, modern vehicles tended to pull it apart. The era of tarmacadam began, and now, few roads, however minor, are not surfaced with bitumen or concrete. Many have been widened, while sharp bends and steep gradients have been smoothed out. Towns and villages have often been provided with bypasses, to relieve congestion and disruption along their streets. Thus all roads have now become motor roads, equipped with the familiar panoply of signs, road-markings, traffic lights, pedestrian crossings and roundabouts.

While all this was going on, it was clear, even by the 1930s, that traffic was growing so fast that the existing network, however well developed, would not be able to carry the traffic which seemed likely to want to use it. Envious glances were cast at Germany, France and America, where new roads seemed to be appearing, and, in response, an entirely new type of road was planned, which was designed exclusively for motor traffic, while pedestrians, cyclists and horse-riders were banned; though the motorway was conceived in the 1930s, it was nearly another 30 years before the first full-length example, the M1, was opened. Outside towns, this comparatively straightforward highway engineering solution has, for the most part, proved successful in providing adequate routes for the ever-rising level of traffic. Even so, the concept was introduced rather timidly, being described as a series of apparently unconnected bypasses; the programme of building was over 10 years old before the government was prepared to claim that Britain now had a network of strategic roads, built for long-distance travel. For the most part these new roads passed through open country; traffic access was restricted to junctions with many miles between them, allowing traffic to flow fairly freely.

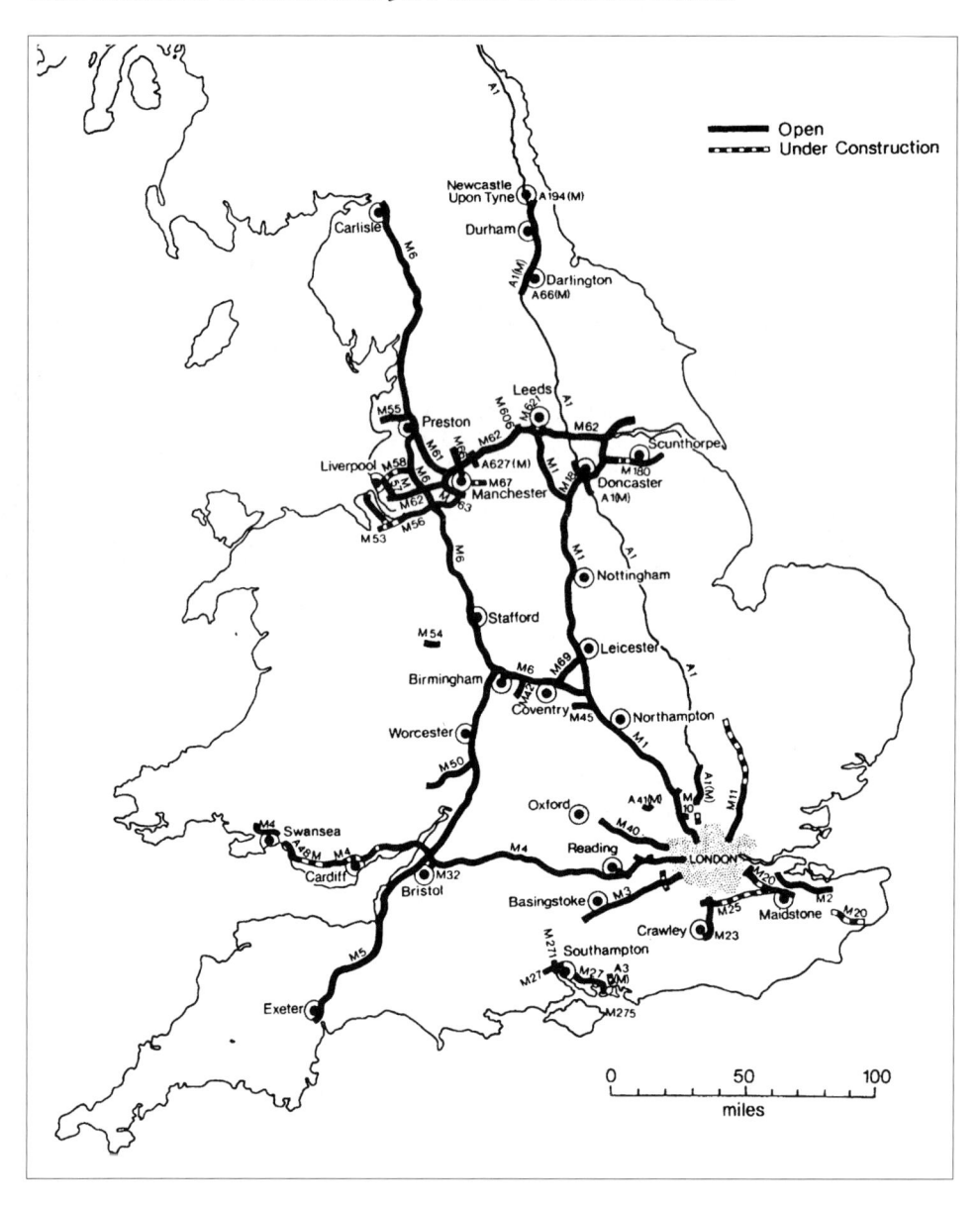

FROM TRACKWAYS TO MOTORWAYS: 5000 YEARS OF HIGHWAY HISTORY

35 The motorway network in 1978. *After Starkie 1982, figure 13.2*

By 1978, 20 years after the opening of Britain's first full-length motorway, the M1, the network was beginning to take shape (35). This intermediate stage of construction gives a good idea of the most urgent priorities in terms of dealing with traffic demand. The need for good links between London and the other major population centres such as Birmingham, Liverpool, Manchester and Leeds are clearly evident in the routing of the M1 and M6, while the M5 to the south-

36 The M74 motorway near Abington, Lanarkshire, completed in the 1990s. It follows the Clyde valley, as do earlier roads and the railway

west was given priority to meet demand for holiday traffic in the summer. The M4 provides the spine of what is now known as the 'M4 corridor', along which modern industries have established themselves in towns such as Slough, Reading, Swindon and Bristol. The M11 to Cambridge was still unfinished, and the M25 was still only apparent in isolated lengths. The network of full motorways is still extending, though at a slower rate than in the '70s or '80s (*36*).

While this network has been largely successful, free traffic flow has been achieved by avoiding urban areas where possible, hence these roads are often described as 'rural motorways'. But, even in the 1930s it was recognised that coping with traffic in towns posed a particular problem. Nevertheless it was assumed that there was a technical solution based on increased road capacity, and grand plans began to appear (Bressey and Lutyens 1938). The subject was

37 Artist's impression of an urban area which has been comprehensively developed to give maximum access to cars, while, at the same time, attempting to provide a satisfactory environment. After Buchanan 1963, 142

controversial from the start; was it really possible to allow all the car journeys which people might want to make in towns, and if so, what would the price be in terms of lost amenity to everyone else?

To address this problem, the government set up a major study. The result was a report, called *Traffic in Towns* (Buchanan 1963). Colin Buchanan and his team showed that a town the size of Newbury could be developed to carry all the motor traffic which might wish to use it, but only by completely redeveloping the centre. Once cities as large as Leeds, let alone London were concerned, even comprehensive, multi-layered redevelopment would still not allow everyone to drive in who might reasonably wish to do so (*37*).

Undeterred, various schemes for urban motorways were started, but public opposition to the disruption and visual intrusion of the massive structures which began to appear, was such that most of the schemes were never completed; instead short lengths of urban motorway have been incorporated, with varying levels of success, into the existing urban fabric (Starkie 1983, 71ff). In order to prevent, or at least control, the inevitable congestion, measures have been taken to limit demand for car travel, such as the provision of public transport, imposition of parking restrictions, and more recently, the introduction of road tolling.

David Starkie's book gives an analysis of the development of motorway policy and its implementation up to the early 1980s (Starkie 1982). A more detailed coverage of all aspects of the subject is being produced for the Motorway Archive Trust; so far, Volume 1 on policy and Volume 2 on technical issues, have appeared (Baldwin and Baldwin 2004, and Bridle and Porter 2002 respectively). Other volumes covering regional issues are to follow.

4

STRUCTURE OF ROADS AND TRACKS

INTRODUCTION

When we drive along a road we are usually aware of the quality of the immediate surface below our wheels; cracks or potholes are rather obvious on a modern 'made-up' road because they are unusual. The surface is smooth and firm, free from bumps and puddles, thus allowing us to travel at high speed. The road remains in good condition for years on end, whatever the weather and despite the daily pounding from cars, buses and heavy commercial vehicles. This chapter is about the long and chequered history of how road-builders learned to make roads which could cope with the traffic of their age, and how difficult it has often proved to keep up with changing demands made by road users.

The principle is fairly easily stated: all routes for travel, from an un-made track to a high-capacity motorway, rely for support on the soil beneath them. In Britain we have a huge variety of soil, sands, silts, clays etc. all of which have different strength characteristics, which can in turn affect how they behave when a load is applied to them. But almost all soils are weakened when they absorb water; the wetter they get, the less able they become to support a load. Thus it is clearly important for road designers to try to keep the soil beneath the road as dry as possible. But something more is needed, because of the particular characteristics of the loads which roads have to cope with, namely that such loads are

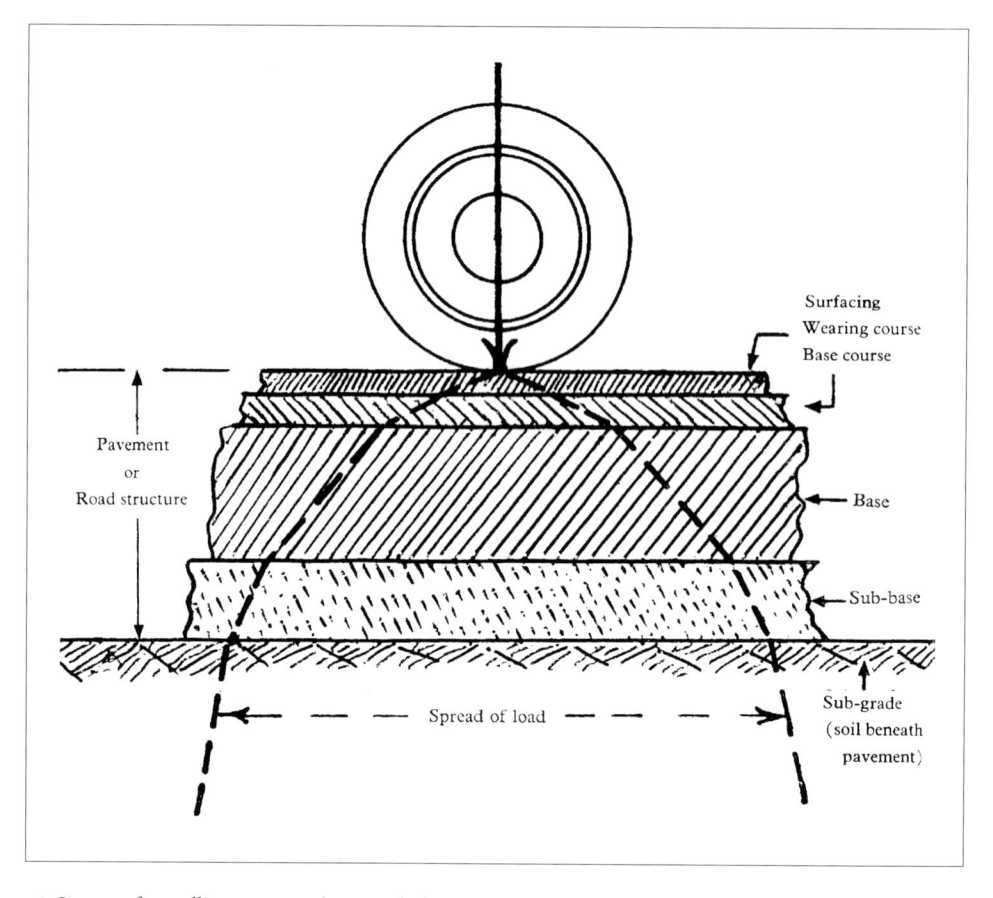

38 Layers of metalling on a modern road, showing how they spread the concentrated load imposed by a passing wheel. Alternative layer identification: 'surface course' for 'wearing course' and 'binder course' for 'base course'. After ARAL 1963, courtesy Quarry Products Association

very concentrated and are repeatedly applied, as feet, hooves and wheels pass along. Under such impacts, soil tends to 'flex' in two different ways: *elastically*, in which each deflection is recovered, and *plastically*, when the soil does not quite recover to its former level. In ordinary soil, with a normal moisture content, the latter is much greater than the former, so that repeated loads, particularly those of wheels, will quickly cause ruts to form. By placing a fairly rigid platform on the soil, the plastic deflection can be made almost negligible; as the load passes, the platform deflects elastically, returning almost to its previous level after the load has passed. The weight of the load is transferred downwards and outwards through the platform, so that by the time it reaches the soil beneath, it has been spread to an extent which minimises damage to the underlying soil (*38*). Ruts still occur, but at a much slower rate.

The material which makes up this platform is almost always called *metalling*: the history of road-making is largely about the search for suitable material for metalling which will enable a road to be hard-wearing, smooth (but not slippery), impervious to weather and economical to lay and maintain. This has not proved to be an easy problem to solve.

We saw in Chapter 2 that during prehistory the absence of heavy wheeled vehicles meant that tracks could be un-metalled, comprising beaten-down earth. In exceptionally wet conditions, timber trackways were constructed from the Neolithic times onwards, but metalling only appeared in the Iron Age, and then only in the form of patching on paths in a few hillforts and settlements where habitation was unusually concentrated. In this chapter we look at the way the use of metalling has developed over the 2000 years since the arrival of the Romans, and describe some of the famous and colourful characters who were involved.

THE ROMANS

The Romans were the first in Britain to use metalling as a normal road-building technique; they usually combined it with their famous *agger*, an artificial embankment on which the metalled road rested, with material for the *agger* coming from drainage ditches running alongside. The basic form of the metalling comprised a foundation of relatively large stones, with smaller cobbles or gravel above to form the running surface (*39*). The passage of wheeled vehicles compacted the surface into a hard, smooth layer. This, combined with the use of a slight camber from the centre to the edge, allowed rainwater to drain to the sides, and thence into the ditches. Besides leading away rainwater, the ditches, along with the *agger*, helped protect the soil beneath the metalling from groundwater, the former by lowering the water table and the latter by raising the road above it.

The average width of metalling on a Roman road in Britain is 22 Roman feet, or *pedes* (the Roman foot, the *pes*, plural *pedes*, is slightly shorter than the Imperial foot, at 11.6in (0.296m)). About 16 *pedes* would be adequate for two wagons to pass, so the average is sufficient to allow some manoeuvring, and a safety margin for other road users on foot or horseback. The average depth of metalling is 20in (51cm), again adequate for good strength. Combined with the use of the *agger* and drainage ditches, the 'average' Roman road would seem entirely adequate for its purpose. However, there are great variations in almost all these features. In an analysis of over 600 excavation sites at which a Roman road was located, it has been found that frequently there was only one ditch, or none at all. Again, the metalling often rested on the natural ground, with no sign of a

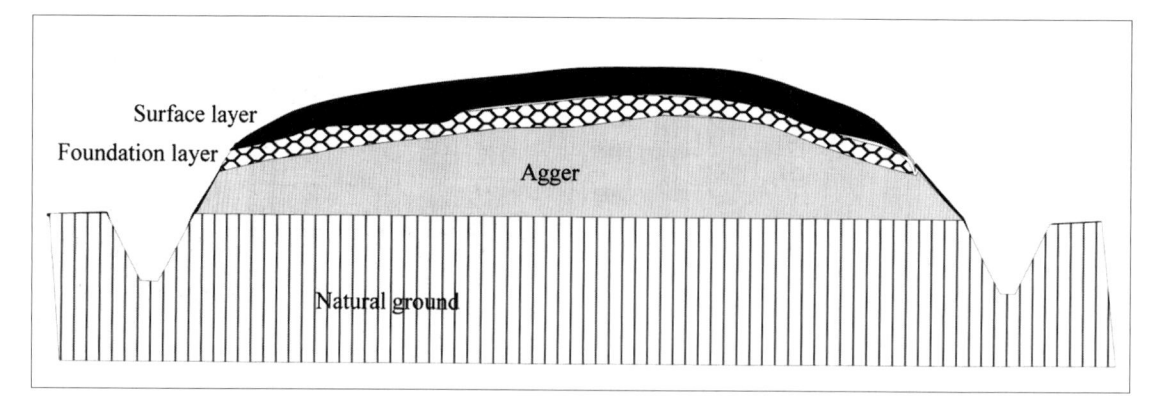

39 Typical form of Roman road metalling, agger and drainage ditches

raised *agger*. Some roads were so narrow that even one wagon would have had difficulty in passing along it, while others were over 60 *pedes* wide, with room for three parallel 'carriageways' (Davies 2002) (*40*). Some form of metalling was nearly always present, though its depth could vary from just a few inches (cm) to over 6ft (1.83m).

Thus it does not seem that Roman road-builders stuck to a rigid formula when laying out their roads, but this does not imply that they had no awareness of what was needed; quite the reverse in fact. The observed variability stems from the variability of soil from place to place, the different volumes of traffic which the roads needed to accommodate, and the passage of nearly four centuries during which the roads adapted to changing needs. Where roads were built on well-drained soil, comprising sand or gravel, or a mixture of these elements, ditches and an *agger* were of less importance, and metalling did not need to be so thick. Road width probably varied from a combination of status and expected traffic volume: for example, Watling Street was, on average, nearly twice as wide as Foss Way, suggesting that the former was a much more important road than the latter during the Roman period. Where traffic was very heavy, metalling would wear out over time and need replacing. Where space permitted, successive carriageways might be laid alongside each other, as happened at Old Ford, where the London to Colchester road crossed the River Lea. However, the usual practice of repair or reconstruction was to place a new road on top of the old one, resulting in a multiplicity of layers. This was especially obvious in towns, where 10 or 15 different road layers can sometimes be seen in an excavation. A good example of the build-up of multiple layers can be seen at the north gate of Silchester (Fulford *et al.* 1997; Davies 2002, figure 49).

STRUCTURE OF ROADS AND TRACKS

40 Roman metalled surface of Stane Street, recently excavated at Westhampnett, near Chichester. Three parallel 'carriageways' of metalling, each about 24ft 6in (7.5m) wide, were found, with ruts which suggest a wheel gauge of 4ft 9in (1.47m), which is almost exactly 5 Roman feet (pedes). S. Jefferey

AFTER THE ROMANS: MEDIEVAL AND EARLY MODERN PERIODS

When Britain ceased to be part of the Roman Empire, in about AD 420, it also seems to have lost the need or ability to build engineered roads. There is no evidence for the use of metalling for several centuries, though no doubt Roman roads continued in use so long as they provided useful routes for travellers. As with prehistoric tracks, often the only indication that a track existed at all is because of linear gaps between groups of pits, such as were found at Lake End Road West, a seventh- to ninth-century Anglo-Saxon site north of Dorney, on the south bank of the River Thames (Hiller, Petts and Allan 2002, 58).

It seems likely that this lack of metalling did not cause major problems because there was little heavy wagon traffic. Comparatively simple roads could cope with feet and hooves, provided judicious diversions were made when any particular track became impassable. Indeed the law provided for the necessity of travellers sometimes diverting onto adjacent land. After the Roman era, the efficient use of metalling does not appear to have become widespread once more until well into the eighteenth century, but, as we see below, the technique was used earlier, albeit with limited success.

In 1947, Sheppard Frere was investigating the eighteenth-century cellars of some shops, fronting on to the north-east side of St George's Street, Canterbury. He noticed that some of the lower courses of masonry were much older than those above, and began an excavation which revealed a Roman bathhouse, upon the floor of which the cellar walls had been founded (Frere and Stow 1983). Though the bathhouse was aligned closely on the modern street, its south-west corner was not accessible because it lay under the street itself. However, in 1982, the laying of a sewer allowed this part and an adjacent Roman courtyard to be excavated too (Bennett 1983) (*41*). There was no Roman street along this side of the bathhouse, but the Roman courtyard levels are represented by several layers of metalling, such as layers 25, 18, 15 and 13. Between these, there are layers of silty material which probably represent flooding from the overflow of a nearby drain used for carrying away effluent from the bathhouse. The last Roman metalling surface is probably layer 10, while 9 was formed by rubble from the collapsed building as the site was abandoned. The lowest Roman level is contemporary with the building of the bathhouse in about AD 200, while the final Roman layer (10) probably dates to about AD 355-60 when the bathhouse was extensively rebuilt. Abandonment is thought to have occurred shortly afterwards.

Layer 8 is described as comprising 2-4in (5-10cm) of black loam, material often found covering the Roman layers of towns, and sometimes known as 'dark earth'. Exactly what was going on when such layers were formed is open to debate, but whatever was happening during this period, there is no evidence that it included the passage of human or animal traffic. Layer 6 is thicker, at 2ft (61cm), with some sign of human occupation represented by oyster shells and animal bones; sunk into this layer is a pit, layer 7, which contained a loom weight of the eighth or ninth century.

With layer 5 we see the first evidence of people moving through the area and causing wear on the ground; though it is un-metalled, the formation of the depression suggests a hollow-way began to form, probably comprising a late Anglo-Saxon street, perhaps the first manifestation of modern St George's Street. Layer 4 comprises eight layers of metalling, laid on the sunken surface of the hollow-way. When this was first laid down is unclear (the excavator suggests late Saxon), but it seems unlikely to have been very effective as rainwater would have

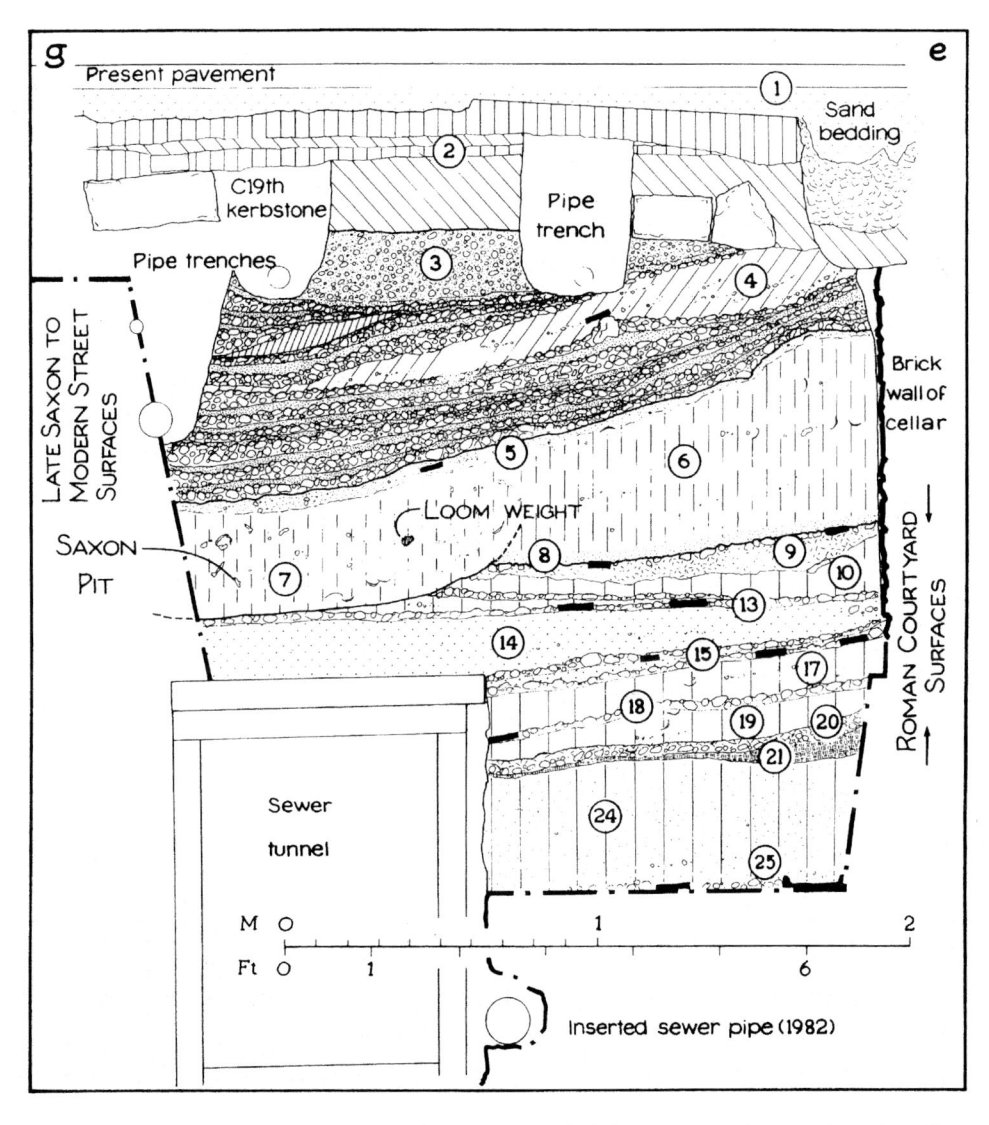

41 Cross-section of excavation at the site of the Roman Baths below St George's Street, Canterbury, Kent, showing layers between the Roman courtyard and modern street level. After Bennett 1983, figure 142

continually collected in the centre of the hollow, reducing the capability of the metalling to carry much traffic without degrading. It does not appear that the hollow was filled (layer 3) until post-medieval times, so layer 4 must represent over 500 years of effort to stabilise the street. Layer 2 is of late nineteenth- and early twentieth-century era, with a tarmacadam surface, while the final layer represents bedding for the present paving stones of the modern pedestrianised St George's Street.

It is clear from Canterbury, and other examples, that metalling may well have been used quite widely in the medieval period, though the way it was applied shows little awareness of what is needed for the construction of an adequate road. Unsuitable material, such as earth and vegetable matter, mixed only sparsely with gravel or larger stones, would be piled haphazardly on the road, which would quickly be worn into ruts by wagon wheels. These would tend to form near the centre, as traffic moved along. The resulting hollow (with a concave cross-section) might be deepened still further by the tendency of residents to deposit their domestic waste onto the street. When yet more unsuitable material was piled in the centre, the shape of the road was temporarily reversed, with a convex surface being formed, which was often so steeply sloping that wagons were forced even closer to the centre of the road, once more causing ruts and beginning the cycle all over again (Kennerell 1958, 184; Lay 1992, 68). This repeated cycle resulted in an inexorable rise in the level of the street, a phenomenon which was a great nuisance. Properties alongside the street would be repeatedly invaded by mud and gravel, washed from the elevated road surface. But the practice continued, despite official efforts to stop it, well into the eighteenth century (Salisbury 1948, 36). Salisbury quotes John Stow as having noted, in the late 1500s, that two churches in London must be very old, because each had to be accessed down a flight of steps, from a road which had originally been built at the same level as the church floor.

Despite the improved materials which are now in use for road surfacing (see below), repairs are still needed from time to time every few years. The fact that such repairs no longer force street levels upwards is because, before any new metalling is laid on the road, the worn-out surface material is removed, for later recycling. The result is that the final street level is precisely the same as it was before the repair began (*42*).

EIGHTEENTH- AND EARLY NINETEENTH-CENTURIES: ROAD ENGINEERS MAKE THEIR MARK

During the eighteenth and early nineteenth centuries, road-building began to catch up with the demands of traffic. From the late sixteenth century onwards there began an increasing use of wheeled vehicles; roads which had survived, albeit inadequately, during the medieval period, began to deteriorate rapidly. Thus, just at the time when people wanted to increase their travel, they found that it was more and more difficult to do so (see Chapter 6). Regaining the Romans' understanding of what was needed to make a good road, took many more decades, and involved contributions from numerous people, both in Britain

42 Modern planing/scarifying machine, removing the worn-out top layers of an asphalt road and loading the material into a lorry, for later recycling

and abroad, especially in France. Three of the most famous British road-builders are highlighted here.

Blind Jack of Knaresborough

John Metcalf (1717-1820), often known as 'Blind Jack of Knaresborough', was perhaps the most colourful. Blinded by smallpox at the age of six, he nevertheless led an active and varied life, earning a living as a fiddler, merchant and smuggler. But at the age of 38 he took up a new challenge, as a road-builder, gaining a fine reputation for his work over almost 40 years (Hogg 1967, 96ff).

During his early life he travelled a great deal, and there seems little doubt that his ceaseless movement, both on foot and horseback, gave him an interest and understanding of what was needed to make an efficient road. In 1755, a turnpike road was being planned between Harrogate and Boroughbridge. One of Metcalf's neighbours had been appointed as surveyor, and, because he was familiar with Metcalf's abilities, agreed to his request to be allowed to build a 3-mile (4.8km) section of the new road. The work was carried out to the satisfaction of the sponsors, with Metcalf seemingly showing good organisational skills as well as an understanding of the particular problems of building in low-lying ground in the Ure Valley; he purchased quarries of good-quality stone, built an access road to the site, and made sure his workers were well fed and properly accommodated nearby.

Metcalf was a contractor rather than a designer, though he had the confidence to press his own ideas during negotiations. In particular he seems to have shared with the Romans the belief that a road should be driven as directly as possible from origin to destination, with intervening problems, such as boggy ground, being dealt with by employing engineering techniques. When such ground was encountered, he advocated the use of brushwood, held together in bundles and laid beneath the road metalling. Although this technique was used by the Romans, it is reasonable to credit Metcalf with its re-invention. If the depth of soft, waterlogged soil is sufficient, the road effectively floats on a raft of timber, upon which metalling can be spread to provide a running surface. This use of brushwood by Metcalf is all the more creditable because such material had often been used previously, but in a highly ineffective manner, as a means of repairing or resurfacing roads; in air the wood quickly rots, leaving a void which disrupts whatever other material has been placed, whereas the brushwood raft rests within the water, and is preserved by the starvation of oxygen.

One further example demonstrates his understanding of soil. He was responsible for a road to be built across an area largely composed of clay. It was normal practice to allow traffic to pass over roads during construction, but he was aware how weak clay could be and closed off the road until the surface was laid. He offered overnight accommodation to travellers who were delayed by the need to make a diversion. In all Metcalf seems to have built over 200 miles (321km) of road, earning himself an enviable reputation as a reliable, skilled and innovative highway contractor.

Thomas Telford (1757-1834)
Thomas Telford rose to become the leading road, bridge and canal builder of his age, and one of our most famous engineers (Rolt 1985). Such epithets as 'The Colossus of Roads' and 'Pontifex Maximus' ascribed to the poet Southey, may seem overblown, but they capture the scale of his reputation. His work in the Scottish Highlands and the Holyhead Road are referred to in the previous chapter. Though perhaps best known for spectacular bridges, viaducts and embankments, his views on road-building were also monumental. He felt it was necessary to have at the base of his roads a solid and immovable foundation, comprising large stones, carefully placed by hand. This technique is known as 'pitching'. He

specified that on a levelled ground surface stones should be placed so that their rounded end was downwards, and their longest side facing across the road. For a wide road, in the centre stones should be 10in (25cm), gradually reducing until at the side they were 3in (7.6cm) deep. Thus the camber was formed by the foundation stones. The tops were to be broken off to make a level surface, and the spaces filled by hammering in smaller stones. He thus created a fairly smooth surface, upon which would be laid smaller irregularly shaped stones, which would be further split by the hard wheels of horse-drawn vehicles and then bedded into a solid running surface (Law 1855, 97). He certainly recognised the importance of drainage, using ditches to keep down the water table, cambers to lead surface water into the ditches, and culverts to carry existing water-courses beneath the road. But he viewed the heavy foundation as essential to minimise the impact of vehicle wheels on the underlying soil. The Romans often used this approach where large stones were plentiful, predominantly in northern and western areas of Britain; elsewhere they were happy to found their roads on cobbles, or even gravel (Davies 2002, 58). Nearly 1800 years after Roman road-building began in Britain, this issue was very much alive, with Telford's approach being opposed by a school of thought which held that hard foundations, far from being the ideal, were in fact a positive danger to the stability of the road; this was the view put forward and applied by John McAdam.

John London McAdam (1756-1836)

In contrast to both Metcalf and Telford, John London McAdam's parentage conferred on him the status of a gentleman, a social position which enabled him to counteract the rather humble image of the road surveyor (Reader 1980, 23). He seems to have obtained his knowledge and theories about road-making from extensive travels, at his own expense, and by careful observation and questioning of those involved. He was forthright and self-confident in expressing his views, so that when he was appointed surveyor of the roads round Bristol in 1816 he had already acquired a considerable reputation (McAdam 1819).

He set out a simple principle of road-building; namely that the whole purpose of the road structure was to protect the underlying soil from getting wet, because moisture reduced its capacity to carry a load (McAdam 1825). This idea was already becoming recognised by the early nineteenth century, but it was McAdam's design for the road structure itself which carried his name, though at the time it caused controversy. He advocated a layer of carefully selected stone; they should be of irregular shape and of weight no greater than 6oz (170gm); this meant a maximum diameter of about 2in (5cm). These stones were laid to form a layer no more than 10in (25cm) thick. The action of hard wheels and horse-shoes would split off small fragments of the stones at the surface, and force these fragments into the small voids between the original stones, eventually forming a hard, impervious layer. A slight camber ensured that water ran to the edge, and good drainage meant that, once at the edge, it was carried away. Drainage also ensured that the water table was kept well below the road structure, thus ensuring that there was a sufficient layer of dry subsoil to support the road.

What many engineers, including Telford, could not accept was that such a thin layer of road material could be laid directly on the ground surface; they wanted a solid foundation to keep the whole road as rigid as possible. McAdam argued that such rigidity was a menace to the road because there needed to be some 'give' in order to preserve the structure. Contemporaries found this hard to accept. Surely, he was asked at a Parliamentary Enquiry on the Highways of the Kingdom in 1819, ' ... you would prefer to build a road over a firm rocky surface than a bog?' Not so, he replied, the rocky foundation, being so rigid, would ensure that the road material was pulverised to dust, while, over the bog, the road would have both strength and flexibility to survive the impact of wheels. He claimed that so long as a man could walk on a bog, a road could be build directly upon it. He described a road he had laid between Bridgewater and Cross, in Somerset, which was built over a 'morass', on which travellers in coaches could see ripples in the water in ditches alongside, caused by vibrations from the road, and that these disturbances were sufficient to break young ice which had just formed in winter. Adjacent to this length, the road was built on rock, and he had found this was more expensive to maintain than that built over the morass ' ... by a factor of seven to five' (McAdam 1819, 24).

He described how he always insisted that any large stones, above 6oz in weight, placed in an existing road structure which needed repair, should be 'lifted' and broken up, the pieces then being relaid. Besides his view that a hard foundation was itself injurious to the surface layer, he also pointed out that the large stones used in such foundations did not remain in position, but moved over time, causing disruption to the road above. He described a road in which, at great expense, a layer of paving stones had been laid flat, and the road surface layer spread upon them. When he instructed that these should be taken up, it was discovered that many of the paving stones were now on end, acting as levers which pulled apart the road above.

Given that Telford was so meticulous in his instructions about the laying of large stones in the foundations, and McAdam was saying that wherever he found large stones in the foundation of a road he would have them dug up and broken into small pieces, this disagreement could hardly be more clear-cut, and it took a fair degree of self-confidence (or arrogance) on McAdam's part to hold his views so trenchantly and consistently. Yet he had practical experience to back up his claims and, as he was offering a cheaper solution, he was much more in demand than Telford as a road-builder. Thus, it is his name which was attached to the smooth surface obtained when small, irregularly-shaped stones are battered by hard wagon and coach wheels, namely a *macadamised* road.

IMPROVING ON TELFORD AND MCADAM: DEVELOPMENTS DURING THE NINETEENTH AND EARLY TWENTIETH CENTURIES

Problems with macadamised surfaces

Macadamised surfaces continued in use on many roads, major and minor, well into the twentieth century (*23*). Although macadamised surfaces were an enormous improvement on the haphazard deposits of stones and rubbish which had preceded them, serious problems remained, for both road user and road-maker. In ideal conditions, with a certain amount of moisture, such particles could help to 'bind' the stones together, but in wet or dry weather the limitations of the method became very obvious; when wet, macadamised surfaces became muddy, requiring regular brushing by 'lengthmen', who were each responsible for a particular stretch of road. These men were also responsible for filling ruts and cleaning ditches. In dry weather the soil particles became dust clouds when disturbed by wheels or hooves. On major roads this was alleviated by watering; for example, cast iron pumps have been found at Charvil and Twyford in Berkshire, part of a series along the Bath Road to supply water for this purpose (Babtie 1998, 5). So, during the nineteenth century, the search was on to find an ideal, all-weather road-making material, a search which continues to this day.

What was needed was a binder which worked irrespective of how wet or dry it got. In addition it needed to be hard-wearing, cheap and easy to lay. Nowadays we also require our road surfaces to resist skidding, suppress spray and limit tyre noise. This has not proved an easy problem to solve and experiments continue to this day.

Tar and tarmacadam

We are familiar with asphalt road surfaces, commonly called 'black-top', which are made with a mixture of bitumen or tar, sand and stone aggregate, but it took over a century from the McAdam era before the method was usable. Tar is a byproduct of timber or coal processing. Prior to the nineteenth century it was produced by charcoal burners, and was in widespread use for waterproofing, particularly in ships. But the cost went down when coal-gas began to be popular for lighting. This gave an opportunity to experiment with its use as a binder on roads; tar was heated to reduce its viscosity and then poured onto the stone road surfaces. Because of the renown of John McAdam these were widely known as macadamised surfaces, so, when tar was added, it was natural to call the result *tarmacadam*. Even though modern road surfaces use bitumen, rather than tar, the name has become commonly used for a black-top road surface. In its shortened version, *tarmac,* it is used as a collective name for the taxiways and runways of airfields, though, of course, many of these are nowadays made of concrete. A further irony is that, while John McAdam had a commercial interest in a tar works, he was not involved in any experiments to use tar for road-building.

The material began to be used on footways (such as on Margate Pier in 1822), and later on streets in Gloucester and Cheltenham. As the warm tar percolated down between the stones, it formed a binding which came to be known as *grouting macadam*. It was often spread so that it formed a thin layer on top. An alternative was to mix the stones and tar before laying, giving rise to yet another variation called *coated macadam*. One problem with a pure tar surface was that it could become very slippery, so sand was tried to alleviate this. There were other problems too; tar can be very slow to set, but when this has eventually occurred the material can then become brittle and prone to cracking. Even so its use continued into the 1920s.

Bitumen and asphalt

Bitumen is a byproduct of oil refining whose main output is petroleum. Because of the high level of production of petrol for vehicles, bitumen is relatively cheap, and has taken over from tar as the main binder in modern road surfaces. However, bitumen, known originally as *pitch* (the modern name may be derived from the older one via *pitchumen*) can occur naturally, and has been known as a useful waterproofing element long before the advent of large-scale oil refining. However, natural bitumen deposits are not pure, but mixtures which also include sand and small stones, in varying proportions. These mixtures are called collectively *asphalt*; it turns out that such mixtures greatly enhance the strength and durability of bitumen, and, when deliberately mixed, as they are today, form the basis of most modern road surfaces. Thus it is conventional to distinguish the natural deposits as *native asphalt* from the deliberately created one, which is known as *manufactured asphalt*. When either material is made suitable for spreading on surfaces it is sometimes called *mastic*.

Deposits of native asphalt have been known for thousands of years, and have been mined to provide waterproofing. For example the Romans operated mines in the Jura Mountains near Neuchâtel and Seyssel, while in Tudor times Sir Walter Raleigh used Trinidad Lake asphalt for caulking his ships. The lake, near the western end of the island, covers an area of about 100 acres (40ha), and is in places said to be 300ft (92m) deep. It can support the weight of a person walking on the surface, and the light railway which takes material from it, but any hole dug in the surface will fill up and disappear in the space of 24 hours (RRL 1962, 31). The material is clearly viscous, but under an impact shows that it is, at the same time, brittle; a hammer can be used to smash the surface into fragments, after which, if the hammer is laid on a nearby area of undisturbed surface, it gradually sinks from sight.

Owners of lakes and mines containing asphalt were keen to find new markets for their product, and during the nineteenth century efforts were made to employ it in road construction. While natural asphalt showed the way, it became obvious that nature could not be relied upon to provide the ideal combination of the constituents. A better result could be obtained by starting from scratch and doing the mixing artificially under controlled conditions.

Manufactured asphalt

This process is called *manufactured asphalt*; when trials began in the late nineteenth century the product was derisively described as *artificial asphalt* by producers of native asphalt, relying as they had always done on the tradition that natural materials would be best. It was well into the twentieth century before manufactured asphalt was competitive in price; not only was it necessary to experiment with individual constituents, bitumen, sand and aggregates, each of which is variable in its durability, but suitable plant needed to be developed for mixing them together, transporting the resulting asphalt to site and laying it on the foundation layers.

Cement and concrete

Cement is derived from burnt limestone; when mixed with sand and gravel it becomes concrete. The addition of water activates the cement to form a chemical binder, analogous to tar or bitumen. Though the process is very ancient, being used for roads by Cretan, Egyptian and Greek civilisations, its main use was in building. The Romans made extensive use of cement in arch construction, but introduced a new and important variation; by mixing a volcanic ash from Pozzuoli near Naples, the concrete could be made hydraulic, so that it would set underwater. This enabled bridge piers and harbour works to be constructed with greater strength and structural integrity. However, perhaps because of its expense, it was used sparingly in road construction. A dramatic exception is a huge concrete layer beneath Foss Way as it approaches Roman Lincoln. This formed a levelling course which enabled the road and adjacent buildings to be built over a waterlogged flood-plain of the River Witham, at the same height as the bridge which carried the road over the river itself. A small area of the upper surface of this concrete layer can be observed today beneath the floor of St Mary's Guildhall (Davies 2002, figure 28).

Though cement and concrete were known to the Anglo-Saxons and Normans, it does not seem to have been used in road metalling again until the nineteenth century. In 1828 Telford experimented with concrete as a foundation medium on the Holyhead Road in North London, but does not seem to have been satisfied with the result because it was not used again.

This may have been because of the limitations of the material available at the time. Burnt lime on its own has limited efficiency as a cement; modern cement, in which clay is added to burnt limestone before it is re-burnt and then powdered, was only invented four years earlier, by Joseph Aspidin of Wakefield in Yorkshire. He called his product *portland cement* on the spurious, but marketable ground that its appearance resembled the structural limestone found on Isle of Portland. Twenty years after its invention, Portland Cement was used as the binder for a concrete base on the Strand in London, on which was placed a surface of granite setts (see below). Various other experiments took place during the nineteenth and early twentieth centuries, though it was usual to spread a layer of asphalt on top, to improve skid resistance and to give the concrete some protection from a tendency to crack as the material expanded and contracted with temperature change. In the 1920s, the introduction of flexible joints reduced stresses and consequent cracking, and many roads began to be made entirely of concrete, giving rise to the familiar, regular thud as vehicle wheels cross each joint.

Flagstones, setts, cobbles and blocks
An alternative to seeking some way of binding stones together is to form the road with prepared blocks. The Romans used flagstones on occasions, while cobbles could often be found in medieval and post-medieval streets. Blocks could also be made of concrete, or formed from timber. Difficulties with binders meant that blocks were still popular well into the twentieth century, but they proved far from ideal; though they were often hard-wearing, they could be very slippery when wet. Consequently most have now been replaced by asphalt or concrete (*43, 44, 45*).

DESIGNING MODERN METALLING

Though many of the developments described above proved adequate for horse-drawn vehicles and the comparatively few motor vehicles which were using the road in the early years of the twentieth century, the rapid rise of the number and weight of vehicles powered by internal combustion engines (see Chapter 6) demonstrated that, yet again, road technology was not keeping up with demand. In many countries a combination of theoretical analysis, laboratory experiments

STRUCTURE OF ROADS AND TRACKS

43 Reconstruction of Middleton Road, Manchester, in 1948. Block paving is being replaced by a cement-bound base and asphalt surface. (This and the next two photographs are by the City Surveyor's Department, Manchester. *Courtesy ICE*)

44 Barber Greene carpeting machine laying asphalt at Middleton Road, Manchester. The company name is often used generically

45 Asphalt road surface being laid at Middleton Road, Manchester. Heavy road-rollers have always been important, to compact each layer while it is still warm and soft. The machine on the right demonstrates that, by 1948, diesel had largely displaced steam as a motive power; even so, the term 'steam roller' continues in popular use, both as a noun and a verb

and full-scale trials was put in hand to find a design for metalling which could cope with modern traffic.

In Britain much of this work has been done or supervised by the Road Research Laboratory (now the Transport Research Laboratory (TRL)). It was set up in 1933, at two sites in West London, before moving progressively to its present site in Crowthorne, Berkshire. From its founding, the laboratory began to apply scientific methods to the development of road-making materials, and studied different ways of preparing and laying them. Though much could be learned by laboratory testing – subjecting materials to controlled wearing procedures – the ultimate test would only come by laying a variety of alternative specifications on a real road and observing the results. Vehicle counts would give an accurate record of the traffic which used the road, climatic conditions such as temperature and rainfall could be recorded, and core-sampling of each type of material would show how it was standing up to the impact of the wheels which passed over it. The first series of trials (comprising 700 specifications of bituminous surfaces) was laid in 1939, along a 1-mile (1.6km) section of the Colnbrook Bypass, part of the A4 in Buckinghamshire (RRL 1962, 240).

Using results from this and many other full-scale trials across the country, RRL produced a series of design guides called Road Note 29 (*Table 1*).

TABLE 1 Relationship between soil type, drainage condition, expected traffic (heavy commercial vehicles per day) and required construction depth

SOIL TYPE	DRAINAGE	DEPTH OF CONSTRUCTION INCHES (MM)	LIGHT TRAFFIC UP TO 150	MEDIUM TRAFFIC 150-4500	HEAVY TRAFFIC OVER 4500
Heavy clay	Good	19 (480)	▓		
		24 (610)		▓	
		34 (860)			■
Silt	Poor	Compensate with additional measure	Supporting the road on piles, floating the road on brushwood, or digging out and replacing unsuitable sub-grade soil may compensate for poor drainage and allow the above figures to be used.		
Silty clay Sandy clay	Good	11 (280)	▓		
		14 (360)		▓	
		21 (530)			■
	Poor	16 (410)	▓		
		19 (480)		▓	
		28 (710)			■
Sand or sandy gravel	Good	8 (200)	▓		
		11 (280)		▓	
		14 (360)			■
	Poor	11 (280)	▓		
		14 (360)		▓	
		20 (510)			■

The table has been constructed using information in the second edition of the guide, for flexible, i.e. asphalt pavements (RRL 1965; Salter 1994, 57ff). The first column identifies the type of soil beneath the road; for convenience some standard geological terms are used to identify soil, though in practice highway engineers test the strength of the soil over which the road is to be built by using a standardised method such as the California Bearing Ratio (CBR) to obtain a more precise prediction of how the soil will behave (Salter 1994, 66). The second column separates sites where drainage methods can ensure that the water table does not come within 2ft (60cm) of the bottom of the road structure (good), from those where such measures are impracticable (poor).

The third column gives recommended total depth of metalling for each of three categories of predicted traffic. For simplicity, only the total thickness of metalling is given in the table, though the design guide specifies various layers for the road structure; at the bottom is the base, sometimes supported by a lower layer, the sub-base, on which are laid the base-course and wearing course. The sub-base is usually composed of mixed aggregate, the base uses aggregate and cement (or bitumen) mixes, while the two top layers are composed of asphalt, i.e. mixtures of bitumen, sand and aggregate (*38*).

The remaining columns show traffic levels in heavy vehicles per day. The traffic levels are those predicted to be using the road during its design life of 20 years. Only heavy vehicles are included in this design guide; these are taken as vehicles with an unladen weight over 30cwt (about 1.5t). The reason that only the number of heavy vehicles need be considered is that tests have shown that the damage caused by wheels is roughly proportional to the fourth power of the load; thus a single axle on a heavy vehicle, loaded to the usual maximum of 10t, has a damaging effect which is 60,000 times greater than the average car axle, loaded to perhaps 0.9t (Salter 1994, table 3.3).

The table shows how modern practice adjusts the road design to take account of soil, drainage and traffic. Testing has demonstrated the variable strength of different types of soil; the design guide shows how this knowledge has been applied to road design. When conditions are ideal, with the soil beneath the road being sand, gravel or sand/gravel mixtures, with well-drained situations and light traffic, metalling need only be 8in (20cm) thick; while at the other extreme, on a difficult site with poor soil (silts or clays), bad drainage and heavy traffic, the road has to be more than four times as thick, with further special measures put in place first. Research continues to improve materials and the way they are laid, to ensure that modern roads are able to cope with the increasing volume and weight of the traffic which uses them.

Flexible or rigid?
The design guides also give recommendations for building roads using concrete (these are usually referred to as *rigid,* while roads built with asphalt are called *flexible*). There is much competition between the industries which supply and lay these two distinct types of road-making material, with the different properties of each being vigorously promoted. Rigid pavements are more expensive to lay, but last longer than flexible ones. Thus, which is cheaper depends on how future costs are discounted to the present time. But other considerations are important.

For example, it is difficult to lay a concrete road so that it is as even to drive on as a flexible one, giving rise to more vibration; on occasions it has been necessary to put an asphalt surface layer on top of a concrete road previously intended to carry the traffic directly. Rigid pavements can also become slippery, requiring artificial grooves to be introduced before the concrete sets; this can give rise to tyre noise. The advocates of rigid pavements point to modern laying techniques which can bring the initial cost closer to that for flexible ones, while supporters of the latter demonstrate new ways of treating the surface to reduce skidding, spray and tyre noise. Thus the arguments ebb and flow, so it seems likely that we shall see both types on new roads for the foreseeable future.

MINOR ROADS: NOT AS STRONG AS THEY LOOK

The foregoing section refers to major roads, such as motorways and trunk roads which are designed to carry large flows of traffic with a significant proportion being of the heaviest commercial vehicles. But they are only a small part of the total length of the road network, which also includes 'A' or 'B' or 'unclassified' roads (see *Table 2*).

TABLE 2 The length of different categories of roads (km). *DfT Transport Statistics (Great Britain)*

YEAR	TRUNK (A)	CLASS 1 (A)	CLASS 2 (B)	CLASS 3 (C)	UN-CLASSIFIED	TOTAL (EXCL. M/WAYS)	MOTORWAYS
1909	-	-	-	-	-	282,380	-
1923	-	37,383	23,720	-	224,285	285,389	-
1947	13,181	31,410	28,498	77,788	143,735	294,582	-
1959	13,401	31,744	28,329	78,653	158,573	310,700	13
1975	15,240	33,088	27,606	80,156	173,949	330,039	1,975
2000	15,101	34,974	30,200	84,624	225,340	390,239	3,467

Many of these, particularly those in the 'unclassified' category are often referred to as *minor roads*. They have not usually had the degree of care and investment that the major roads have had; they may appear as strong and smooth as major ones, but this may be deceptive.

Nearly all these roads have a well-laid surface of asphalt, but a potential problem may lie beneath this layer because many minor roads have only limited

a) Engineered Road

Fine material
Hardcore
Shoulder
Drain

Pavement

SUBSOIL

b) Unengineered Road

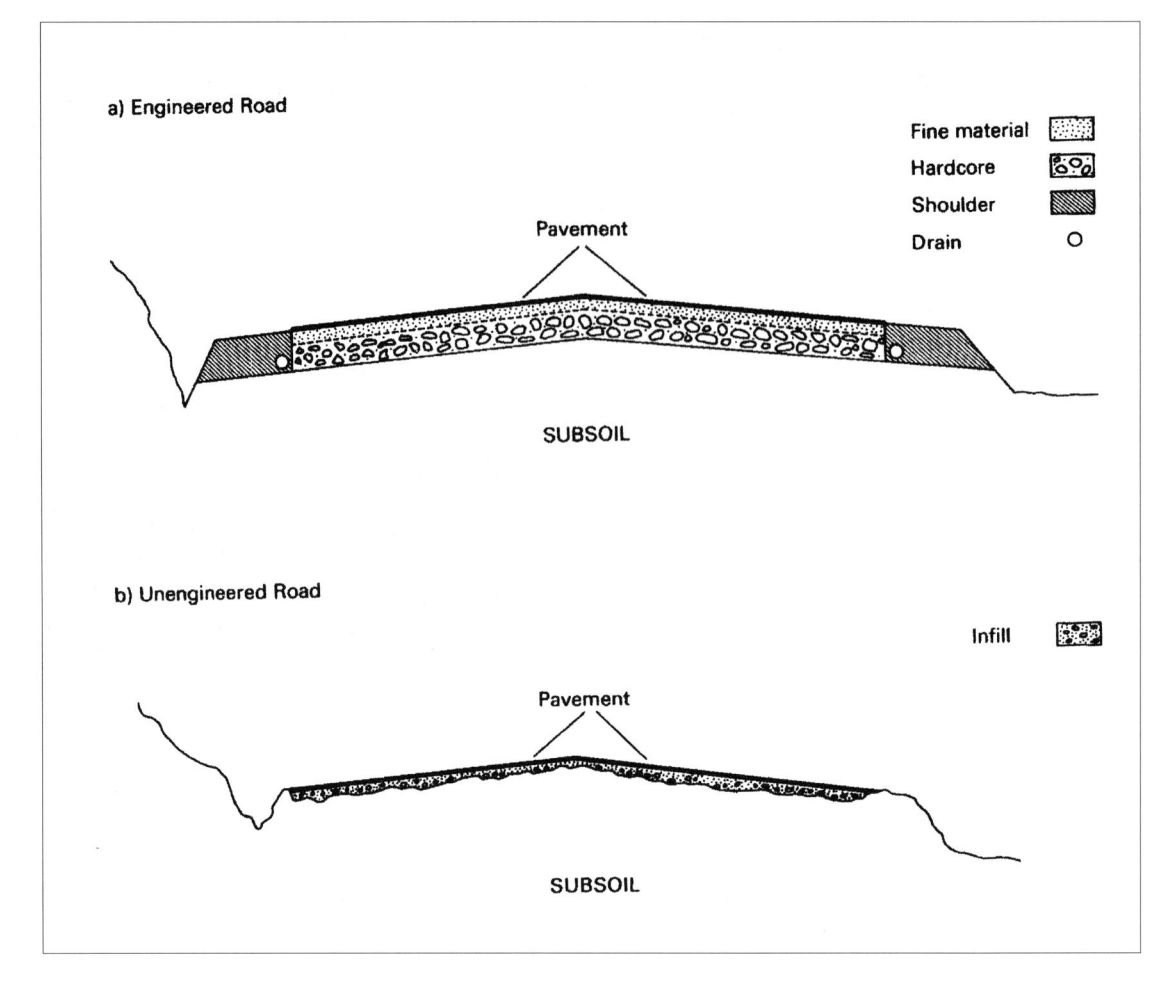

Infill

Pavement

SUBSOIL

46 Diagram showing the difference between minor roads which are (a) fully engineered and (b) unengineered. *After Edwards 1984, figure 2.1*

foundation structures, or even no foundation layers at all. This means that the whole road is much weaker than it looks. The two forms of construction have been observed by Gareth Edwards in a study of minor roads in Wales (Edwards 1984) (*46*). Though his study concentrated on three limited areas of central Wales, there is no reason to suppose that the roads he analysed are not typical of other parts of Britain. Item (a) shows a properly engineered road, capable of carrying a good deal of traffic, with occasional heavy vehicles.

However, in his study, Edwards found that many roads were similar to item (b), hardly more than surfaced cart tracks, or lanes with a minimum of stone metalling beneath the tarmac surface. He shows how the passage of vehicles can cause the surface to flex, and crack, and then become 'crazed'. Rain water can

STRUCTURE OF ROADS AND TRACKS

then penetrate from above, further weakening the surface layer and penetrating through to the soil beneath, causing it to lose what strength it would have had when dry. The effect of frost can exacerbate all these effects. In addition, the poor drainage allows water to accumulate alongside the road, penetrating beneath the surface and contributing to the reduction of its carrying capacity.

As traffic levels, particularly of heavy vehicles, rise, the surface deteriorates quickly. However, resurfacing can only be a temporary solution, because problems soon arise again. Only comprehensive rebuilding, with an appropriate foundation, can allow the road to perform efficiently.

Similar shortcomings to those described above are not confined to rural roads and lanes. Relentless traffic growth means that, even in well built-up areas, neglect for only a few decades can necessitate major reconstruction (*47, 48*).

47 Even the busy High Street, Sandhurst, Berkshire (A321), required major reconstruction involving several weeks of closure, after some neglect

48 Adhesion mats being laid between road layers during the reconstruction of High Street, Sandhurst, Berkshire. The mats give stability to the numerous layers beneath a modern, busy road

BRIDGES

Finally in this chapter we look at bridges, which are among the most prominent and impressive features to be seen on our roads. Their development and methods of construction are beyond the scope of this book; for information on such topics as Roman stone bridges, Roman culverts and timber bridges, medieval bridges and motorway bridges, see O'Connor 1993, Davies 2002, Harrison, D. 2004, and Bridle and Porter 2002 respectively.

Though many bridges are major features in their own right, they should be seen as an integral part of the road network. Before the Roman period, travellers probably relied on fords, stepping stones and ferries for crossing waterways. After the arrival of the Romans, with their engineered road network, water crossings were gradually provided with bridges or culverts. Major estuaries such as the Humber and Severn (below Gloucester) continued to operate with ferries. No doubt some Roman bridges continued in use during Anglo-Saxon times, but many crossings must have reverted to their former fords. However it seems clear that, as the medieval period progressed, much more effort went into bridge construction than was devoted to roads, so that most of the routes shown in the Gough Map of 1350 (*17*) had proper bridges in place at river crossings. A more detailed look at one particular route, that from London to Gloucester, shows how the availability of bridges could affect the route people take at any given time.

In Roman times, the road to Gloucester crossed the Thames at Staines, continuing south-west and then west until it reached Silchester. After passing through this important town, the route continued via Cirencester, crossed the Cotswold Ridge at Birdlip and continued on to Gloucester, where the bridge over the Severn allowed access to Wales. As can be seen from figure *17*, this route is far from direct, but may have been chosen for engineering reasons; it has the advantage of needing only one Thames crossing, thus minimising the amount of road-building in waterlogged areas of the Thames valley. By contrast, the Gough Map shows a completely different route to Gloucester; leaving London via Uxbridge, the road then passes through Oxford and Burford, a course followed by the modern A40. Though the route avoids the Thames valley altogether, it does instead involve a steep ascent and descent at the Chiltern Hills near High Wycombe.

Even by the time of the Gough Map, there were several middle Thames bridges in place at, for example, Wallingford, Reading, Henley, Marlow, Windsor and Maidenhead (Harrison, D. 2004, 22, 56). Travellers could now reach Gloucester by a more direct route than going via Silchester or Oxford, by crossing the Thames at Maidenhead, Henley and Wallingford, then joining up with the old Roman line to reach Gloucester via Cirencester.

Towns grew prosperous because of their bridges, but were also vulnerable to competition. For example, John Leland noted in 1542, after visiting Abingdon, that the building of a Thames bridge there had caused the Gloucester Road to pass through the town rather than Wallingford, as it had done previously (Chandler 1993, 34).

The bridge was built in 1416, later than many other Thames bridges (*49, 50*). After several people were drowned attempting to cross via the ferry, the local people eventually gave up trying to persuade the lord of the manor and the monastic authorities to build a bridge, and decided to do the job themselves, sponsored by a local guild, and supported financially by local benefactors. The whole event was recorded in a colourful poem by one of the guildsmen, Richard Forman. In describing the enthusiastic application of the volunteers to the task in hand, he says:

> The mattock was manhandeled right wele a whyle.
> With spades and schovells they made such a noyse,
> That men myght here hem thens a myle...

49 Bridge over the Thames at Abingdon, Oxfordshire. Some parts of the fifteenth-century original structure are incorporated within later additions

He goes on to describe what amounts to a giant picnic for those at work and others watching (Pollard 2003).

The fact that so many bridges seem to have been built in the medieval period perhaps gives an over-optimistic impression of the situation confronting the traveller. As with roads, bridges needed constant maintenance, but, while roads might deteriorate, forcing pedestrians, wagoners or riders alike to seek local diversions, a neglected bridge could collapse completely, forcing travellers to divert many miles or consign themselves to the expense and often danger of a ferry ride. J.J. Jusserand points out that the method of financing bridge-building and repair was just as ad hoc as that for roads, leading to many examples of bridge failure. He describes the history of one example, Berwick Bridge across the Tweed. This is first heard of in 1199, but subsequently collapsed frequently, on each occasion being rebuilt, sometimes in timber, sometimes stone. After a severe inundation it collapsed again in 1294, and remained in ruins until 1347, travellers in the meantime coping with expensive and unreliable ferry operators. A system of dues on users of the harbour was devised for financing a new bridge, but this fared no better than its predecessors, with more collapses being reported (Jusserand 1889, 34).

STRUCTURE OF ROADS AND TRACKS

50 Section of Abingdon bridge, as it crosses a side channel of the river Thames, viewed from the east

London Bridge was of major importance, and is perhaps the most carefully studied. The Romans almost certainly had a bridge across the Thames at Southwark, close to the site of present-day London Bridge (the spur of gravel at this point has made this a suitable crossing point from Roman times onward). The layout of roads and streets clearly suggests the presence of a bridge, but absence of any masonry evidence points to the bridge being made of timber (an impression of what the bridge may have looked like can be seen in model form at the London Museum). The bridge almost certainly had numerous arches, as the river Thames was over 300yds wide at that time, and may have had an opening section in the middle to allow boats to pass. At the end of the Roman period the bridge probably fell into disrepair, but documentary evidence suggests that a replacement, probably still made of timber, may well have been in place by the reign of King Aethelred II (978-1016) (Pierce 2001, 20). It was not until 1176 that work commenced on the famous Old London Bridge, built of stone, with its numerous houses and archways. Tolls were used to raise money, but income from these could easily be misappropriated so that the bridge became impassable; for example, in 1282 Edward I was forced to raise a national tax to get the bridge open again (Jusserand 1889, 31). Wardens were eventually appointed to be responsible for the work, and they could call on other sources of income to supplement that from tolls. By 1382 this comprised money from rents, not only from properties on the bridge itself (of which there were nearly 140), but from other properties within London and from farms outside it. This enabled the employment of a permanent staff of craftsmen, clerks and rent collectors (Pierce 2001, 84).

Besides Berwick and London, Jusserand gives many examples of bridge failures during the medieval period. It may well be that choice of route for travellers may often have been based, not just on whether particular river crossings were provided with a bridge, but whether or not they were usable at any particular time.

Bridge collapses are not unknown, even in the modern era, but nearly all of these occur during construction. The structure is vulnerable at this time, but when all components are in place, the ability of arches and girders to transfer load to solid piers and abutments makes a completed bridge very resilient. Provided the fabric is properly maintained, bridges can survive for many centuries, even with far greater weight and volumes of traffic crossing them than was originally envisaged (*51*, *52*).

Such resilience can lead to over-confidence however: John Crane recounts an occasion in 1945 when the 120-ton capacity trailer made by his family firm in Dareham, Norfolk, broke through the bridge over the river Ure on the A5 at Boroughbridge in Yorkshire. The trailer was carrying an 80-ton stator, and was

51 Complex series of bridges at Berwyn, north of Llangollen, Denbighshire, on the river Dee. Telford's early nineteenth-century Holyhead Road crossed a tributary on a bridge which stands immediately behind the mid-century railway bridge. A later road bridge across the main river was threaded through the arches of the earlier structures

being hauled by one Diamond T tractor unit and pushed by another. The leading tractor and front trailer bogie had reached the central pier, but the rear bogie broke through the bridge deck and crashed to the river below, taking the rear tractor with it. There was time for the crew of this vehicle to jump clear, so there were no casualties, but the episode only strengthened complaints about damage to roads and bridges caused by heavy loads. The bridge was first built in the sixteenth century, and it is perhaps a tribute to Tudor era engineers that it was not this structure which collapsed, but an eighteenth-century addition to widen the carriageway (Crane 1991, 69). By using regular inspections and maintenance, and by controlling the axle loading of vehicles on the road, modern bridges are

52 Before Telford's Holyhead Road, the river Dee was crossed near Trevor, Denbighshire. The present bridge, dating from the seventeenth century is seen, with Telford's famous Pontcysyllte aqueduct in the background

rarely damaged by vehicles crossing over them. The danger comes rather from vehicles on roads which pass underneath; when a lorry collides with the pier of a railway bridge, trains are stopped from passing overhead until the structure has been inspected for damage.

5

THE SHAPE OF ROADS

INTRODUCTION

The previous chapter discussed how a road is constructed, and how metalling and drainage are used to protect the soil beneath from damage. However, much of this structure is hidden from view, so the traveller is unaware of how much, or how little, work has gone into providing the surface along which he or she is proceeding. This chapter looks at aspects of road design which are much more immediately evident, such as gradient, width, curvature and superelevation, all of which determine the volume of traffic a road can carry, at what speed and to what degree of safety. We shall also deal with more subtle aspects of road geometry which affect how the road looks and 'feels' to drive along.

GRADIENT

Introduction
The gradient of a road is the rate at which it rises or falls; for example, a road is said to have a gradient of 1 in 20 if it rises or falls vertically by 1ft for every 20ft horizontally (this being a ratio, the unit of measurement is immaterial). An alternative approach, which gives almost exactly the same result, is to measure

53 Watling Street (A5), passing through the deep cutting at Puddlehill, Hertfordshire. The cutting has been made progressively deeper since the Romans began it, probably in the first century AD

distance along the road rather than horizontally. The former is the preferred definition when a new road is being planned using engineering drawings, but the latter is easier to apply in the field when measuring the gradient of an existing road, and is used in this book. Gradients are sometimes expressed as percentages; thus a gradient of 1 in 20 can be shown as 5 per cent.

For most of our history, road-builders have not concerned themselves much with gradient. In both prehistoric and medieval periods, tracks often followed a 'natural' course, adapting to steep ground by following stream courses, natural terraces or ridges. The Romans had a more direct approach, but seem not to have worried too much unless gradients greater than 1 in 6 were encountered. Only occasionally did they use a technique, now familiar, of putting the road in a cutting to keep the gradient down (53). Considering that many of their roads were intended for wheeled traffic, this might seem rather perverse; while such gradients can be coped with by foot or hoof traffic, driving wagons up or down them requires slow and careful negotiation. The answer is probably that the Romans did not design their roads for high-speed wagon traffic, carrying passengers, but for heavy freight, which would only move at walking speed even on the flat.

Things began to change in the sixteenth century. More trade meant an increase in freight traffic by wagon, though it is doubtful if carters would have provided a sufficient lobby on their own to demand better roads. What was new to Britain was a growing fashion for passenger travel by coach or carriage; yet anyone attempting to make journeys this way found that the roads were bumpy, muddy and steep, so that speeds were often no more than, and sometimes less than, could be achieved on foot (see next chapter). It was pressure from passengers which eventually led to demands for improvements.

Thomas Telford's rationale for selecting maximum gradient

We saw in the previous chapter that improvements in the structure of roads began to be made during the eighteenth century, though it was not until Thomas Telford began to study the problem of road travel that the question of gradient received careful attention. His objective was to build roads along which wheeled vehicles could travel at a reasonable speed, perhaps 10mph, regardless of what sort of terrain the road was passing through. Clearly this was impossible on the current series of turnpikes along the Holyhead Road, particularly as it passed through North Wales, where gradients of 1 in 6 were not uncommon. He knew, from his experience with canals, how to build cuttings and embankments to reduce gradients, but this did not answer the question of what gradient should be chosen as a maximum; limiting gradient using earthworks was expensive, so he looked for a rationale to balance the cost of construction with the efficiency of the new road for carrying traffic. Accordingly his chief assistant, Sir Henry Macneill, began a series of experiments which led to a more rational and scientific basis for decision-making about gradients.

The basic elements of the problem were very familiar (54). The figure shows the forces which act on a coach as it is pulled up a slope (a), along the level (b) and down a slope (c). When a horse-drawn vehicle travels on the level, the horses need to overcome a resistance to motion which comes mainly from rolling friction between the wheels and the road, shown as R. When the coach goes up a slope there is a further resistance to overcome caused by the force of gravity, shown as G. However, when descending the two forces act in opposite directions, gravity helping to counter rolling resistance. On a steep slope, G could be much greater than R, so that, unless braking was applied, the coach would go out of control.

The problem was that braking systems were fairly primitive, often necessitating locking the rear wheels of a coach or wagon. This could damage the road, and in any case would cause delay as the coach slowed down. What Telford needed was to find a maximum gradient at which the force of gravity and rolling resistance were equal; this would mean that a horse-drawn coach could descend a slope at a trot without the risk of losing control.

It was relatively easy to calculate the effect of gravity, at any particular gradient, using trigonometry, but rolling resistance was more complex. There was some drag from the friction on the bearings holding the two axles of a coach, but the main effect came from contact between the wheels and the road; a smooth road produced little resistance, a rough or soft road caused a much higher effect. But to get some actual values for R, Macneill needed to make some practical measurements. He set up a dynamometer between a coach and a team of horses so that he could measure the force the team exerted as it began to pull the coach forward. He found that there was over five times the rolling resistance on a soft, loose surface than on a hard one, and that resistance was twice as high when a coach was travelling at 10mph than at a walking pace (Law 1855, 64ff: Cron 1974, 78).

Telford was then able to calculate that a maximum gradient of 1 in 30, on the hard road surfaces which he intended to lay, would give just the matching of gravity and resistance he needed to allow coaches to travel safely downhill at their normal speed. However, to avoid huge expense in the hilliest areas he was prepared to accept maximum of 1 in 20, suggesting that coach drivers would need to have exercised some caution, though they could still avoid the need for braking. Even at the steeper gradient, the road was a vast improvement on what went before, where gradients could rise to 1 in 6.

Nothing on the scale of the works along the Welsh section of the Holyhead Road had been attempted before, and indeed were not seen again until well into the twentieth century. However, less spectacular, but nonetheless important regrading exercises occurred during the late eighteenth and early nineteenth centuries. Geoffrey Timmins has shown this process taking place in the textile-

THE SHAPE OF ROADS

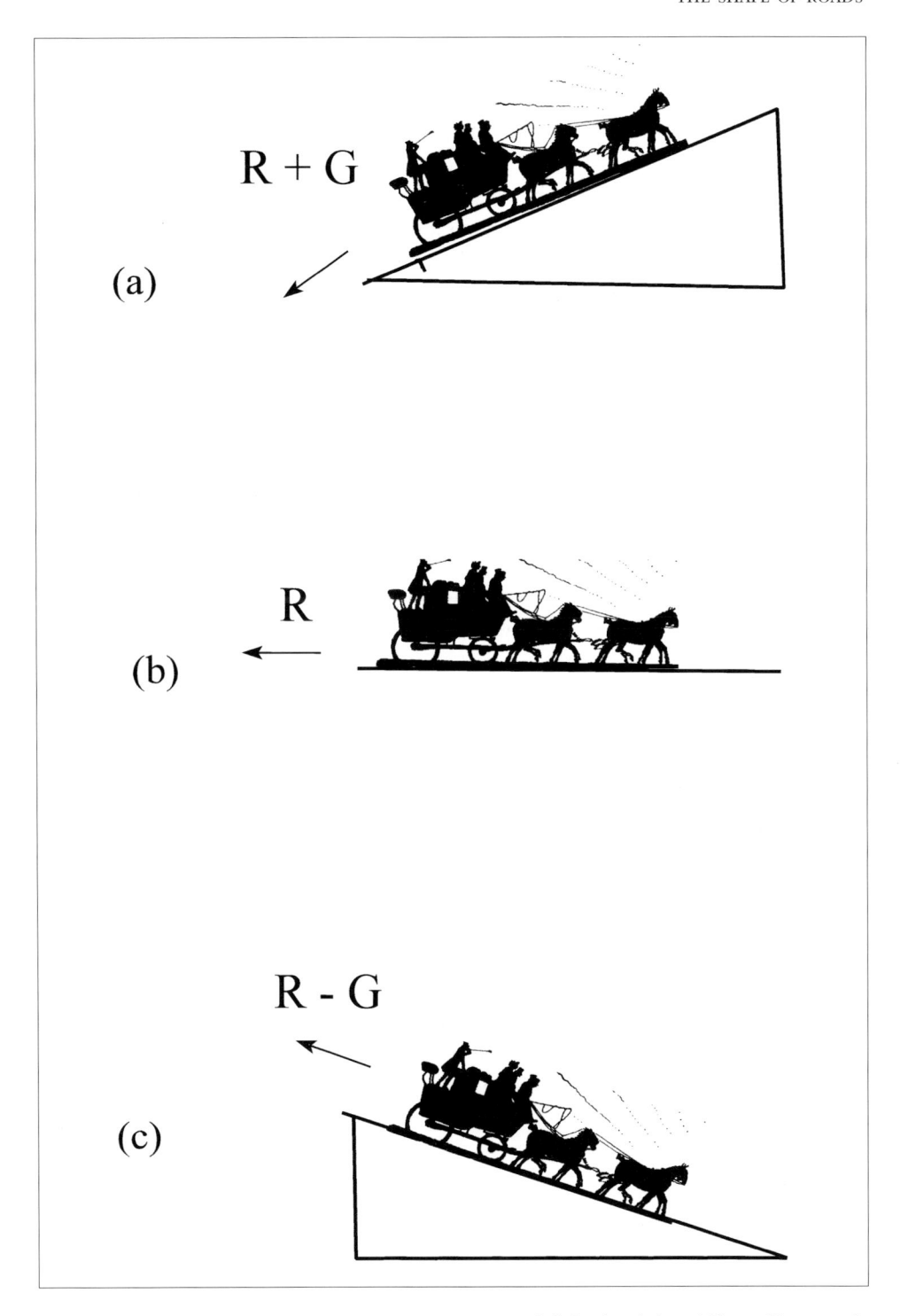

54 The effect of gravity (G) and rolling resistance (R) on uphill, level and downhill travel by a coach and horses, as analysed by Telford and Macneill

producing area of Lancashire (Timmins 2003). By realigning roads to lower ground, gradients could be reduced from 1 in 5 to 1 in 30, though sometimes significant works were needed, including cuttings, embankments and terracing. For example, on the road through Thrutch Gorge in Rossendale, a 10ft (3m) high platform was built to keep the road well above river level.

Gradients in the motor age

All heavy structural work more or less ceased during the late nineteenth century when the railways became dominant for inland transport. Roads tended to become local feeders for stations and goods yards; reduced long-distance passenger and freight movement by road (see next chapter) meant lower toll incomes and less resources available for road improvements. Thus, by the time that the motor era began at the turn of the twentieth century, many stretches of road, both major and minor, still had steep gradients. This led author and publisher Harry Inglis to produce his *Contour Road Book* series, covering England and Wales (Inglis 1899-1907) and Scotland (Inglis 1903). The books contain descriptions of over 1400 individually numbered stretches of road, including details of the gradient to be expected and the state of road surfaces. Both were critical for early motor vehicles, so it was important for drivers to know what to expect on any particular journey. However, some of the author's comments might seem surprising today: for example, when describing Road 880, between Gloucester and Faringdon, he recommends using it as part of the route to London because of its good surface, despite the fact that drivers needed to ascend the 1 in 7.5 gradient of Birdlip Hill, a situation which he himself describes as 'highly dangerous'.

Though the power and controllability of motor vehicles improved greatly as the twentieth century progressed, along with their ability to climb and descend steep hills, pressure to be able to maintain ever higher average speeds led to a renewed programme of road levelling (55). For high-speed roads, such as motorways and trunk roads, a gradient of 3 per cent (1 in 33) has emerged as the maximum allowed in normal circumstances, with 5 per cent (1 in 20) being allowed in very hilly areas (Bridle and Porter 2002, 170). It is interesting that these figures for gradient are very close to Telford's specification for the Holyhead Road, despite the very different traffic conditions being planned for. Whereas he wanted safe average speeds of about 10mph for horse-drawn carriages driving on macadamised surfaces of compacted stones, modern road designers are providing for average speeds of over 70mph on smooth bituminous or concrete surfaces.

55 Works to reduce gradient on Llanfair Talhaiarn – Llansaran road, Conway, N. Wales, in 1925/6. *Kenyon Phillips Ltd., courtesy Institution of Civil Engineers*

ROAD WIDTH

To say that roads vary enormously in width may seem to be stating the obvious; there might seem to be little comparison between a country lane along which two vehicles can only just pass by using gateways or other local wide points, and a motorway with two wide carriageways with hard shoulders, the first perhaps 10ft (3m) wide, the second over 15 times wider. Yet these and all other roads are directly comparable because they comprise one or more traffic lanes running alongside each other, and the width of each of these lanes has hardly changed in 2000 years.

The Romans do not appear to have specified road widths explicitly in terms of traffic lanes, but the concept is clearly implied by the way in which road width was specified. The minimum width of a *via*, a road suitable for vehicles and pack animals, was required to be 8 Roman feet (the Roman foot, or *pes* (plural *pedes*) measured about 11.6in (0.296m)), with 12 *pedes* being required on bends.

This width almost certainly applies to one-way traffic, with a width of 15 *pedes* being the absolute minimum required for two-way flow. This was the width of a tunnel near Pozzuoli in Italy, which, contemporary sources make clear, was intended for two-way movement by wagons (Davies 2002, 70). Thus it might be reasonable to take 10 *pedes* (9ft 8in (2.9m)) as a notional preferred width for a traffic lane. In practice roads varied enormously in width, though 20 *pedes,* effectively accommodating two traffic lanes, is not uncommon.

During the medieval period road width tended to be a rather flexible concept, though there were attempts to regularise it. In Norman times Article 80 of the *Leges Henrici Primi* dealt with highways leading to a city, fortress, castle or royal town. Though most of the article deals with the offence of *forestel* (an assault on a traveller), the width of the road is also required to satisfy three criteria: first that two wagons can pass, second that two herdsmen could just make contact with their goads held at full stretch, and third that 16 knights should be able to pass along unhindered (a rather more demanding requirement than the first two). That the concept of a road is really no more than an area kept clear of obstruction is illustrated by a statute of 1284 laid down that a width of 200ft (61m) should be kept clear of trees for all routes between market towns (13 Ed 1, St 2, c. 5). This great width was required because roads which were not metalled, or only intermittently so, could easily become very muddy and rutted. Travellers were permitted to veer off the more direct line, onto adjoining land, thus effectively widening the road. In difficult situations such widths could extend to over 1 mile (1.6km).

By the nineteenth century, roads tended to run between enclosed areas of land, so that their maximum width was fixed by boundary fences, hedges or walls. Drainage ditches ran along these boundaries, with traffic being confined to the metalled surface between them. For different parts of the Holyhead Road, Thomas Telford specified widths varying from 32ft (9.8m) to 28ft (8.5m) (Quartermaine *et al.* 2003, 19). This gives an average of 15ft (4.6m) for a single traffic lane, which seems generous compared to the Romans; presumably some more room was needed for manoeuvring coaches with perhaps six horses travelling at 10mph. Henry Law gives two further reasons why wider roads should be preferred; firstly, that they avoid wagon drivers following exactly the same line each time, thus causing wear to be concentrated into ruts, and secondly, that a wider road allows more air and sunshine to reach the surface, thus aiding drying by evaporation (Law 1855, 83). He recommends a width of 30ft (9.2m) for roads 'between towns of any importance' with a footpath of 6ft (1.8m). This is the same width as advocated by John McAdam for the road between Bristol and Bath (McAdam 1819, 22).

Though motor vehicles are usually wider than horse-drawn wagons and carts, and travel faster, they are more manoeuvrable and do not require quite so much room. When new roads were being built in the first half of the twentieth century they allowed 10ft (3.1m) for each lane of traffic; for a modern motorway this has risen to 12ft (3.7m) (Bridle and Porter 2002, 186).

Thus the amount of road allocated for a single line of traffic varies from the Roman 'preferred' width of about 10 *pedes* (2.9m) up to about 15ft (4.6m) for the fastest roads in the nineteenth century, while modern lane widths lie between these values.

ROAD CAMBER: CROSS-FALL AND SUPERELEVATION

If instead of looking along the road we look across it, we will usually see that the cross-section is not flat, but cambered. There are two distinct forms of camber, cross-fall and superelevation, which affect the slope of the road's surface from the centre to the edges.

Cross-fall is used to ensure that water runs off the road surface laterally to be collected in roadside ditches or drainage pipes. The Romans usually ensured that roads had some sort of cross-fall, generally resulting in the centre line of the road being higher than the sides. This technique has been used ever since and is an almost universal shape for roads, with a slope of perhaps 1 in 60. During the medieval and early modern periods much greater cambers could arise because road repairs were carried out by simply dumping new material in the centre of the road, where there were more ruts. The result of this was that wagon drivers were forced to run their vehicles down the centre of the road just to avoid being tipped off the road altogether, thus merely adding to the differential wear in the centre and encouraging a repeat of the previous failed repair (Law 1855, 86; Lay 1992, 68). An echo of this past policy may be evident in some present-day urban streets where steep cambers can sometimes be encountered; these seem entirely unnecessary to ensure water run-off, and they can make for some inconvenience to pedestrians attempting to cross and drivers endeavouring to park.

Superelevation, on the other hand, is a comparatively modern concept, originally used on the railways and later on high-speed motor roads. When a vehicle encounters a horizontal curve the first law of mechanics states that it will attempt to continue in the direction in which it is already travelling; a lateral force needs to be applied to get it to turn round the bend. On a railway vehicle, this force is supplied by the rails, which apply pressure on the wheel flanges. On a road it is the friction between tyres and road which supplies this force, once the front wheels have been steered in the right direction. If the combination of speed and sharpness of turn is too great there is a risk of a train leaving the rails or a road vehicle skidding, but even in less severe situations a sharp turn can cause discomfort to rail passengers or vehicle occupants alike. We shall see below how transition curves can be used to alleviate the abruptness of the turn, but some other measure is needed to ensure safety and comfort once the turn is being made. The answer is to raise the outside of the rails or road so that, overall, there is a slope towards the centre of the curve; this technique is known as superelevation. It was first advocated in 1797 by John Curr, who was a 'coal viewer' in a coalmine. He had noted that wagons filled with coal were much more stable going round sharp bends on a tramway if the outer rail was at a higher level than the inner one (Gallagher 2004, 407). The technique was widely adopted on the railways, where speeds in excess of 50mph were commonplace from the mid-nineteenth century, but it was not necessary on roads with speeds of around 10mph; problems caused by sharp bends were dealt with by straightening the road. During the motor age however, as speeds increased towards, and past, the present maximum of 70mph, superelevation has become a standard feature. On new roads, it is usually calculated to provide about 40 per cent of the lateral force, while friction on the tyres provides the remainder, with a maximum value of 1 in 14.5 (Bridle and Porter 2002, 131).

VERTICAL AND HORIZONTAL CURVATURE

Perhaps the most important feature of a road, as regards the speed and safety of travellers is its curvature, whether it be the frequency and intensity of horizontal bends or vertical undulations. Natural topography and human development can both affect the need for a road to take a curved alignment, but it is usually the case that the more curved and undulating a road is found to be, the slower and more carefully drivers must travel; visibility is reduced necessitating care to avoid collisions, and vehicles may need to reduce speed simply to negotiate such features in a controlled manner.

The Romans are renowned for having very straight roads; one theory encountered by the author to explain this style of road-building holds that the Romans built their roads straight because they had not invented steering and were thus unable to take their vehicles round corners. While it is true that there is some controversy over the ability of Roman wagons to steer, it is clear that Roman roads contained bends, sometimes very sharp ones indeed. Certainly long stretches of their roads are remarkably straight, with a series of straight lines making only minor changes of direction at particular points, presumably to correct for errors in surveying the route. However, when steep hills were encountered, the Romans used the technique of a zig-zag course to ascend and descend, necessitating very sharp turns at each change of direction. The use of this technique, rather than a longer diversion with fewer tight bends, suggests that the Romans were not concerned about high average speeds for wagon traffic. Visibility of oncoming traffic would not have been a problem with low speeds, but drivers would have to have treated the steep gradients and sharp bends with caution. Where the Roman line across undulating ground is followed by a modern road, lack of visibility can be a problem (56).

During the medieval period it seems possible that roads got somewhat bendier. We have seen in Chapter 3 that in many cases routes which had previously followed Roman lines began to veer off the direct route to reach communities which had grown up away from the old line; such diversions would not, in most cases, have retained the Roman direct style of alignment but would have followed the local terrain or passed round pre-existing land boundaries, thus adopting the familiar meandering course of many minor roads. However, because of the poor state of the road surface, it seems unlikely that wheeled vehicles would have been

56 View of the A68, north of Corbridge, Northumberland. The road is on the line of the Roman Dere Street, and retains the switchback effect of a straight alignment on undulating ground. There is a risk of an on-coming vehicle being hidden in a dip; consequently the road is more dangerous than it appears

able to go fast enough for such bends to have been the controlling factor on speed and journey time.

Certainly it was the case that, when turnpike roads began to be built in the seventeenth and eighteenth centuries, many still retained sharp bends. However, the demand for more speed by the users of passenger-carrying coaches and carriages meant that a slow programme of bend straightening was begun, in tandem with efforts to reduce gradient (see above).

This process of straightening was somewhat curtailed by the advent of the railways in the second half of the nineteenth century, but began again, with renewed vigour in the twentieth, as motor vehicles made their appearance. Roads with sharp horizontal bends and abrupt vertical undulations, such as when crossing the once-ubiquitous 'hump-back bridge', which had been manageable at 10mph, began to cause serious problems as speeds rose to 30mph and more. As new roads began to be planned and built, there was a need for a more organised approach; what, after all, was a 'safe' bend or a 'safe' undulation? The subject of road geometry was born in the 1930s, as engineers began to debate, sometimes with passion and even venom, the merits of different theories of how the bends and humps of a road should be arranged and how sharp they should be allowed to be.

When a road is designed, its horizontal alignment, or plan, is specified as a series of straight lines linked by curves. Motor roads began to be built like railways, with long straight sections linked by arcs of circles. In order to avoid abrupt changes from straight to curved sections, the ends of each circular arc are linked to the adjoining straight by a spiral, called a transition curve (Bridle and Porter 2002, 124; Gallagher 2004, 413) (*57*).

Railways use comparatively short transitions, and this practice was adopted on the M1, opened in 1956. However, even as the motorway was being built, ideas of how roads should be laid out were changing; a policy of having much longer transitions had been adopted, so that the M4, built 10 years after the M1, has practically no straight sections at all (*58, 59*).

DESIGN SPEED

There is one further element which affects both how safe a road is to drive on and how well coordinated it appears. During the 1950s, RRL examined roads on the Continent and America; amongst the many different aspects of road design which were investigated, the study found situations where vertical and horizontal curves followed one another (Colwill 2004, 676) (*60*). Besides causing unexpected 'blind' spots, this layout resulted in a rather jerky switchback feel

THE SHAPE OF ROADS

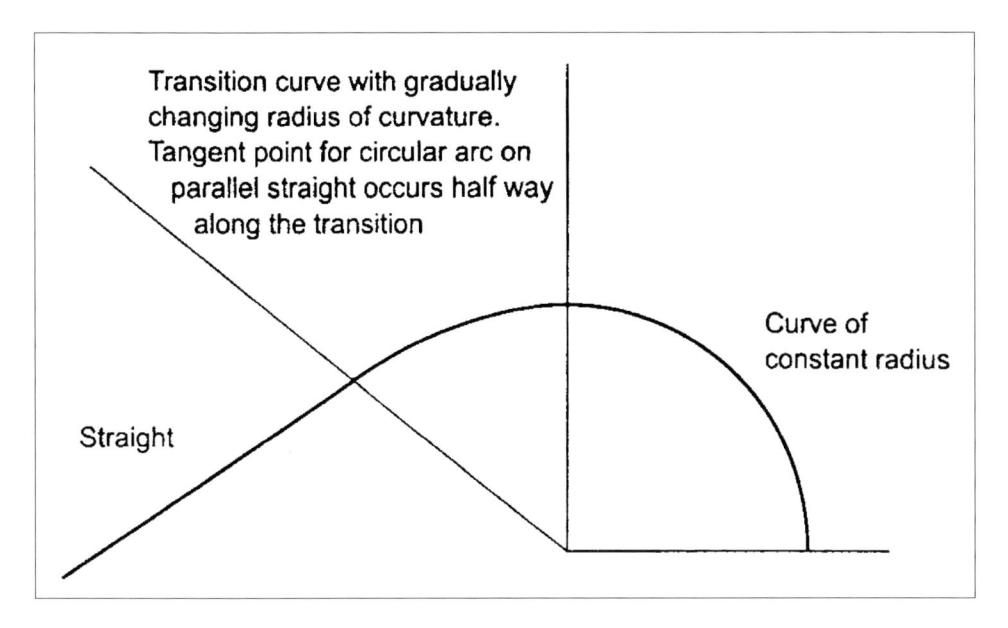

[Diagram showing transition curve with labels: "Transition curve with gradually changing radius of curvature. Tangent point for circular arc on parallel straight occurs half way along the transition", "Straight", "Curve of constant radius"]

57 Diagram of a transition curve, linking a straight section of high speed road with the following curve, thus avoiding an abrupt change of curvature; this is thought to give a safer and more pleasing driving experience. Long, straight sections have been eliminated from modern motorway designs. *After Bridle and Porter 2002, figure 3.3*

to the driver. By ensuring that vertical and horizontal curves coincide as far as possible, a smoother ride is offered, with fewer unexpected situations awaiting the driver over the next hill or round the next bend.

There is one factor which links all the foregoing discussion of curves and superelevation: namely, how fast the driver is travelling. Research can show how far drivers can see round bends and how quickly they react, or how stable a vehicle is when cornering. Obviously these are linked to speed; higher speed gives less time to respond, results in longer braking distances and reduces cornering stability. A great deal of research has been, and continues to be, conducted to assess the effects of speed; road designers need to take account of driver behaviour, weather conditions and vehicle design (Colwill 2004). Once the link with road geometry has been established, actual minimum standards for curvature cannot be fixed without setting a figure for actual speed on the road. This figure is called the *design speed*. On motorways it has been set for decades at 70mph in rural areas, less in urban situations. Note that the design speed is not necessarily the same as the legal speed limit; the latter can be altered from time to time (or even from hour to hour as happens in bad weather or when traffic is congested), but the former is permanently built into the road's geometry. Thus anyone travelling faster than the design speed, whether or not they are exceeding

58 A straight section of the M1 motorway, looking south towards Junction 11 in Hertfordshire

the speed limit, is progressively losing the safety benefit of the features built into the road's design, and, inevitably, running an increased risk of collision or loss of control. Recently, a less rigid definition of design speed is being employed, called

THE SHAPE OF ROADS

59 A section of the M4 motorway, west of Reading, showing the flowing alignment, with no long, straight sections

highway link design, this connects the design speed to the prevailing topography to ensure that roads can be built with geometric standards which are not unnecessarily generous (Bridle and Porter 2002, 175).

JUNCTIONS

The amount of traffic a road can carry is known as its *capacity*, and for normal situations (excluding the effects of hold-ups because of accidents or road-works), the capacity of a road is determined by its junctions. We are all familiar with queues at traffic lights or roundabouts, waiting to leave a side-road or slowing on a motorway as the next junction is approached. Not surprisingly a great deal of work has been done on designing junctions to try and get traffic through

60 Autobahn, Germany, 1937, one of the examples in the RRL study of uncoordinated arrangements of vertical and horizontal curves. *Courtesy ICE*

them as quickly as possible, with elaborate computer programs being used to control traffic lights, careful layout being specified for roundabouts and give-way lines, while one-way traffic systems attempt to reduce the complexity of vehicle movements at the most difficult junctions in an area.

Problems at junctions are not new; stone bollards were used in Pompeii in the first century AD to limit the turning movements of wagons on awkward junctions. We can assume from the shape of some junctions in Roman London (*Londinium*) that wagon drivers would have had some difficulty in negotiating them (Davies 2002, 138).

Junctions were no doubt a problem during the medieval and early modern periods, but it appears that it was only in the motor age that measures such as roundabouts and traffic lights begin to appear.

On motorways and trunk roads, great efforts are made to ensure that traffic does not have to stop; thus junctions have had to be designed to ensure a free flow, at least on the main route at a junction between a motorway and a non-motorway, and free flow on both routes when two motorways cross or merge. This is achieved by carrying one route over the other on a bridge, and so has come to be known as *grade separation* (Bridle and Porter 2002, 187; Gallagher 2004, 400) (*61*). The diagram shows some of the designs which have been used in Britain. Item (a) is a standard two-level junction, where traffic leaves or joins the major road on slip roads, which lead to a roundabout, above or below the motorway. These are by far the most common junctions on our motorway system, and have a fairly straightforward design, usually with the roundabout being formed by two separate bridges. Far more complexity arises when both routes are required to have slip roads for entering and leaving; various designs for these are shown in (b) to (f). Item (b) is the classic clover-leaf design, originating in America; its advantage is that it requires only two levels, as for (a), and therefore minimises construction complexity, but on the other hand it requires a great deal of land. There is also a serious operational flaw with the basic design. To understand this, follow north bound traffic. As the bridge is approached, traffic joins the road by means of a slip road from the west-bound carriageway. Shortly after the bridge, traffic wishing to travel eastwards leaves. Thus in a short distance traffic carrying straight on encounters vehicles entering, and trying to merge immediately before another point where traffic wishes to leave, creating a potentially confusing and dangerous mix of manoeuvres. It is far better practice to take traffic away from the main road before allowing more to join. Item (c) achieves this with the basic clover-leaf, although creating more complexity, by adding merge lanes alongside the main routes. Item (d) is a development of (a), with the east–west road passing beneath the north–south one, while the roundabout lies between them, thus forming a three-level design; this approach is used on the junction

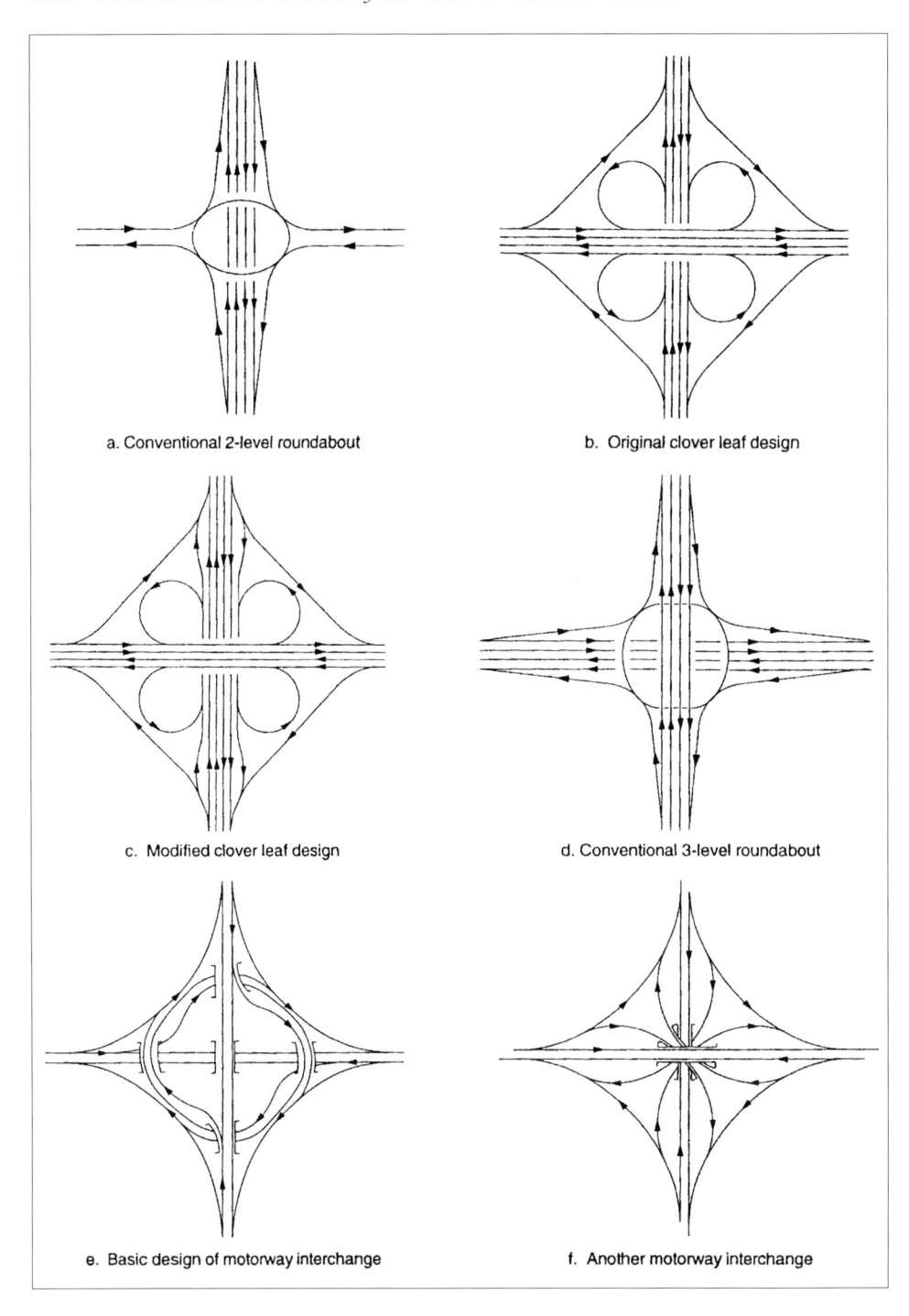

61 Six junction layouts, where grade separation is used to increase capacity on motorways. The designs show the trade-off between the amount of land required and the vertical height of the structures. *After Bridle and Porter 2002, figure 3.14*

between the A45 and A46 south of Coventry. Item (e) allows free-flow for all traffic, as in (b) and (c), but, by employing four levels, reduces the amount of land required; the most famous of these is at Almondsbury in Gloucestershire, where the M4 crosses the M5, but another can be seen near Reigate, Surrey, where the M23 merges with the M25. Finally, item (f) is another multi-level motorway-to-motorway junction design, used where the M3 crosses the M25 near Thorpe, also in Surrey.

6

USING THE ROADS

INTRODUCTION

In the previous chapters we have looked at the history of where and how roads have been built in Britain. But what roads are like ultimately depends on how they are used, so in this chapter we shall look at the means by which people make journeys; in transport jargon this is called their *travel mode*; such modes include travelling on foot, on horseback, as passengers in horse-drawn coaches and carriages, as cyclists, as passengers in buses or minibuses, and finally as drivers or passengers in cars. Of equal importance in road developments are modes for conveying freight; thus we shall, in parallel, be considering the early use of pack animals, then ox- or horse-drawn wagons, steam-powered vehicles and lorries, through to lorries powered by petrol or diesel. We shall also look at the dangers of travelling on roads and the means used to try and reduce them.

Roads and traffic can engender strong emotions, and we end this chapter by looking at some illustrations of what are often ambivalent attitudes towards them.

TRAVELLING ON FOOT

In Chapter 2 we saw perhaps the earliest record of journey-making in Britain, with the discovery of Mesolithic footprints in areas such as the Severn Estuary. Walking continued to be the main mode of travel during the prehistoric period, and remained so in the Roman, medieval and early-modern eras; furthermore it was often the mode of choice even for those who could afford an alternative.

Two examples illustrate this last point. Firstly, Samuel Pepys often walked along the Thames from Whitehall to inspect dockyards at Woolwich, Deptford and Greenwich, during the 1660s and '70s, distances of 10 miles (16km) or more; he enjoyed the exercise and scenery, even when his job as Secretary of the Navy Board entitled him to hire a coach at public expense (Tomalin 2002, 138). Secondly, John Metcalf, the road-builder Blind Jack of Knaresborough, though a competent horseman, did much of his widespread travelling on foot, by choice. He claims to have won a bet with his friend Colonel Liddell that he, on foot, could outpace his friend in a private carriage, as they both returned from London to Yorkshire in 1739. In the event, Metcalf won his bet by reaching the inn before Liddell, on all but the first of the six legs of their journey. Even in May, on as important a route as the Great North Road, the coach frequently got bogged down, needing the efforts of Liddell's servants to free it (Hogg 1967, 54).

It is clear that walking was quite a normal method of getting about, whatever the length of journey, and, of course, for many, it was the only mode they could afford. The coming of the railways, trams and horse-drawn omnibuses, during the nineteenth century, offered much cheaper travel opportunities than had been available hitherto, so there was less incentive to make long journeys on foot. Walking was still the norm for short journeys; this only began to change with the advent of the motor vehicle. From then on, these two modes began to clash and compete for public attention and support; motorists cried 'give us freedom' while pedestrians cried 'give us protection' (Cooke 1930, 120ff; Sprey 2004).

Even today, when a large proportion of the population has access to a car or public transport, walking is still a common means of making journeys (over 30 per cent of trips in Central London). Greater volumes of vehicular traffic has increased the risk of casualties to those on foot; recognition of this by government and local authorities has led to the development of many of the 'traffic calming' measures now to be seen on many town and city streets (*62*). Yet the continuing importance of walking as a normal mode of travel for short journeys is often ignored or thought to be of low priority. There might perhaps be an image problem here. People who travel on foot are usually described as 'pedestrians'. It is unfortunate that the same word can be used as an adjective to describe something as lacking in imagination or as uninteresting. It may be that

62 An early Zebra crossing. The stripes were added to the well-established Belisha crossing in 1951 to give the crossing greater visibility to drivers. *Courtesy Living Streets*

63 A Street Audit taking place in Bakewell, Derbyshire to assess the potential for an improved environment. *Courtesy Living Streets*

politicians and transport specialists fear being linked with the metaphorical image rather than the practical one. Awareness of such attitudes led the Pedestrians Association, founded in 1929, to re-brand itself in 2003 as *Living Streets*, focusing on the wider issue of making our town and city streets safer and more pleasant for all those who use them and live alongside them (*63*). Recent recognition of the physical and social benefits of walking, such as, for example, children going to and from school, has raised the profile of this mode of travel, though the car is proving to be a formidably competitive mode even for short journeys.

The foregoing has concentrated on walking as a travel mode, a means to an end of getting from start to finish of a journey. There is, of course, a well-established tradition of walking for recreation and observation. This seems to be a phenomenon which emerged in the second half of the eighteenth century, perhaps as a reaction to the greater opportunities to travel in a wheeled vehicle. We speak today of rambling; then it became known as the 'Walking Tour'. This was the age of Wordsworth, Coleridge, Hazlett and Shelley, though perhaps the first to expound the virtues of such activities was Thomas Penman, who toured Scotland, Wales and the Lake District between 1769 and 1773 (Marples 1960, 33). Even late in the eighteenth century, male walkers had to overcome a certain prejudice that such activity was not befitting a gentleman. Women suffered an even stronger resistance, but some were determined to ignore such views; Jane Austen not only walked for pleasure but included characters in her novels, such as Elizabeth Bennett and Anne Elliott, who did the same. But it was probably Dorothy Wordsworth who did much to popularise long-distance walking for women. In her *Memoirs* she describes a journey with William in 1794, when they walked 18 miles (29km) from Kendal to Grassmere, followed later the same day by 15 miles (24km) from Grassmere to Keswick (Marples 1960, 90).

Interest and enthusiasm for such activities have continued to this day. It is reasonable, however, to distinguish what is essentially a recreational activity from walking as a mode of travel. While Jane Austen's character Elizabeth Bennett walked for pleasure, she was also prepared to do it for important journeys too: having ascertaining that the carriage-horses were unavailable, but being determined to visit her sister Jane at Netherfield, she decides to walk, assuring her mother that she could make the 3 miles there and back before dinner (*Pride and Prejudice* Chapter 7). People making short, ordinary journeys on foot gain many of the physical and social advantages enjoyed by ramblers, while at the same time employing a convenient and economical means of making routine trips as part of their daily lives (*64*).

64 Pedestrians on Holland Park Avene, Notting Hill, London, out for exercise, to visit shops or for any of a myriad other journey purposes. This busy street would also have been busy 2000 years ago, as it lies on the line of the main Roman road running westwards from Londinium

TRAVELLING ON A HORSE OR IN A CARRIAGE

Until the sixteenth century long journeys would normally be made on horseback for those who could afford to own or hire a horse. For men it was regarded as more 'gentlemanly' to ride, rather than sit inside a horse-drawn vehicle; while there does not seem to have been such a social stigma for women, riding was often preferred. There was an undoubted advantage of travelling under cover in a wagon, but progress was slow, uncomfortable and uncertain. The vehicles were heavy, unsprung and unsteered; they are sometimes referred to as being of 'Luttrell type' because of the illustration in the pages of the Luttrell Psalter. The discomfort of the vehicles was magnified by the state of the roads on which they ran; these were often poor, being hard and uneven in fine weather, muddy and often impassable in bad. Though there was some status for aristocratic women in travelling in such a vehicle if it was richly decorated, for most people it must have seemed little better than being treated as a piece of baggage.

About the middle of the sixteenth century, things began to change. This can perhaps be dated from 1564 when, according to the antiquary John Stow, Walter Ripon made for Queen Elizabeth I a 'coche' of Continental design, with some degree of suspension and a steerable front axle (Piggott 1992, 151). In 1571 the Queen attended the opening of Parliament in such a vehicle, and a fashion began, which Stuart Piggott describes as 'soon becoming a craze' for travelling in coaches. While the aristocracy could afford their own vehicles, coachmen and horses, public service stage-coaches began to operate for those who could not afford ownership but could afford the fare.

As we have seen, road-building took time to catch up with demand, but had sufficiently improved by the late eighteenth century that there began what some have called 'The Golden Age of the stage-coach' or as Cecil Aldin describes it, the age of 'The Romance of the Road' (Aldin 1986).

This golden age was comparatively short-lived; by the mid-nineteenth century long-distance journeys were transferring to the railway. The impact of these changes on a specific area can be seen from M.J. Freeman's study of passenger travel in South Hampshire (Freeman 1975). He summarises the changes by calculating the total of stage-coach movements in and out of each town (or

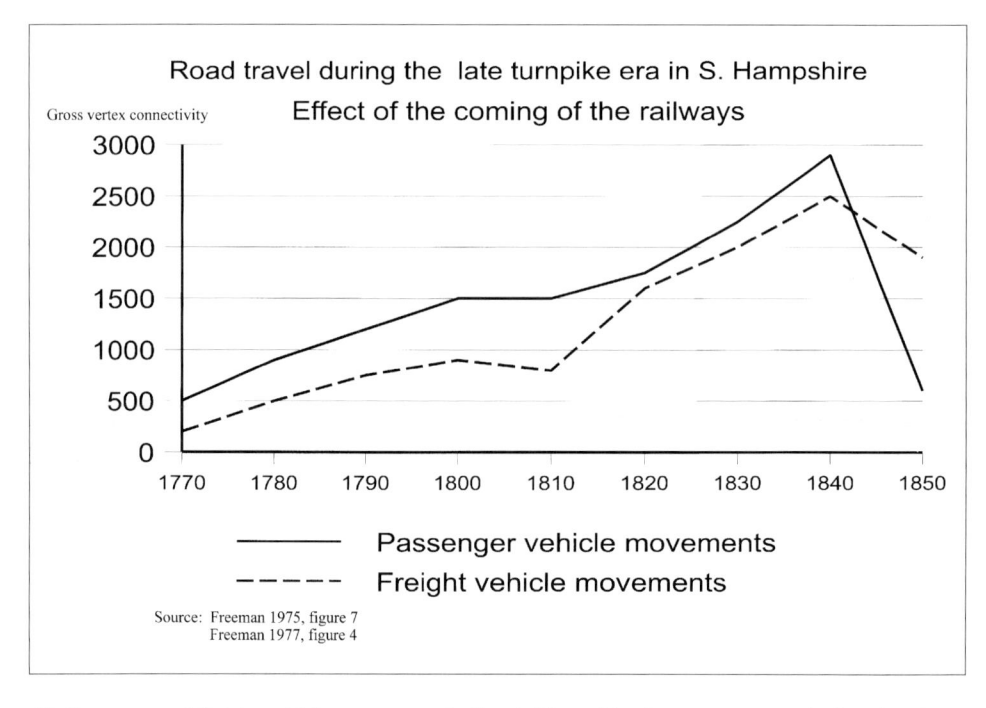

65 Passenger and freight vehicle movements in South Hampshire, between 1770 and 1850, showing a rising trend until the arrival of the railway in the area in 1840. *After Freeman 1975 and 1977*

vertex) on the network, during each year, and then summing the results to obtain a gross vertex connectivity graph (65).

As can be seen, in South Hampshire (solid line in the figure) there were two distinct periods of expansion, a gradual one between 1770 and 1810, and a shorter but much more rapid one between 1823 and 1840. At this point there were, for example, 15 scheduled stage-coaches a day, each way, between Southampton and London, with a capacity of 170 passengers each way. Adding in links to other destinations gives a daily inflow/outflow passenger capacity of stage-coach services, to and from Southampton, of over 1000. An abrupt decline began in 1840 with the opening of the full length of the London–Southampton Railway, though the graph shows that by 1850 there were still more services than there had been in the 1770s, with shorter routes continuing to fill gaps left by the expanding railway.

Though the timings of expansion and contraction varied across the country, the overall pattern was the same. At just the point in time when the railway age began, the road network was probably in the best condition it had ever been, probably surpassing what the Romans had achieved. Transfer of traffic from road to rail meant there was less demand for roads to be maintained to a high standard, and less money available to do such work. Nevertheless, standards were kept up sufficiently to allow use of the network by the earliest motor vehicles, which began to make their appearance at the end of the nineteenth century.

TRAVEL IN TOWNS BEFORE THE MOTOR ERA

During most of our history, for those who could not afford their own horse, or horse-drawn carriage, which of course meant most people, walking was the only option. But towns could be very congested; besides pedestrians, there were private carriages, horse-riders, animals on their way to market, and the mass of other activities which took place on a typical town street. Beginning in the sixteenth century, in large towns, it became possible to make short journeys on vehicles which were licensed to ply for hire; if anything, congestion increased still further, as two-wheeled hackneys and light four-wheeled carriages competed for passengers. By the nineteenth century, in London, larger vehicles, running on tram tracks, began to appear; these could offer very cheap fares, because one horse could pull a vehicle with 20 passengers; when the vehicle ran on rails, two horses could carry 50 people inside and on top of a double-decked vehicle (Taylor 2002, 12).

A form of travel which became popular with those who could afford the fare, was the sedan chair (Hart 1962). By the nineteenth century this mode of travel had become associated with travel for the aged or infirm in places such as Bath, but for two or three centuries before, it was regarded as a normal transport mode in cities. It had the unique advantage that users could travel, under cover, and if desired in complete privacy, from within their own home to a room at their destination.

FREIGHT MOVEMENT: PACKHORSE OR WAGON?

There seems little doubt that, for most of our history, any ordinary goods which had to be moved were carried by hand, while logs or large stones were hauled on sledges or rollers. At some point in prehistory, perhaps as long ago as the Neolithic, a new means of freight transport began to be used, namely the packhorse. Each capable of carrying 240lb (109kg), and linked in lines of 30 or 40, packhorses provided an excellent means of transporting goods. In the sixteenth century, two- and four-wheeled wagons began to appear. Eventually wheeled vehicles took over the job of moving freight, but so versatile were packhorses that they continued in use until the early years of the nineteenth century. This transition has been studied by Dorian Gerhold, who shows that, so finely balanced were the relative advantages of the two modes of operation, they were both used, often by the same carrier, for over a century (Gerhold 1993). While wagons could carry heavy, indivisible loads of several tons, provided material could be packed into appropriate panniers, packhorses had several advantages. For one thing, packhorses were smaller and therefore needed less provender; even so they could often carry more weight than a draught animal could pull. When roads were rough or steep they could travel much faster, achieving 150 miles (220km) a week, as against 120 miles (180km) for a wagon, thus not only completing more revenue-earning journeys in a given time, but enabling carriers to charge a premium for quicker delivery. As a result packhorses were used for bringing fish from ports, such as Workington and Lyme Regis, to London from the sixteenth to eighteenth centuries. On the other hand, wheeled vehicles were, by the sixteenth century, in widespread use in agriculture, so that operators who were involved in both carriage and farming could increase the utilisation of wheeled vehicles. As the eighteenth century drew to a close, a different way of operating long-distance transport began to become popular, in which horses were changed at regular intervals; this enabled carriers to operate by night as well as by day, raising daily distances to 40 or 50 miles (64-81km) per day.

Early horse-drawn vehicles were often two-wheeled affairs, though far heavier than the pony-and-trap combinations which can still be seen today. These would be long vehicles, pulled by five or six horses in single file. However they were unstable, particularly when going downhill, and difficult to load. Four-wheeled wagons initially called 'waggons' eventually took over in the sixteenth century; their popularity was greatly enhanced by the introduction of efficient steering, a feature imported from the Continent.

Four-wheel wagon operation was well established by the time of the arrival of the railways. In the previous section M.J. Freeman's gross vertex connectivity graph for passenger operation in South Hampshire, from 1775 to 1820, was shown. He has also analysed freight operation in the same area (Freeman 1977); his results (hatched lines) are also shown in figure 65. As can be seen, there is a similar, though not identical, pattern. Competition from rail does not seem to have had so drastic an effect as it did for passenger services; after 1840 the carriers were able to transform their operations to provide local services, or by feeding goods to the nearest railway siding, while some of the old routes serving markets continued much as before.

A specialised form of freight comprised written material, letters, official documents or messages. Until the seventeenth century ordinary people needed to make private arrangements for the movement of such material, relying on relatives, friends, or business colleagues to transport and deliver light packages of this type. A good example of how this system worked in the fifteenth century is provided by the many surviving letters written by members of the Paston family (Barber 1999). Their country seat was in Norfolk, but they had no difficulty in keeping regular contact with members of the family in London and even on the Continent, throughout the turbulent Wars of the Roses. Only the monarch (or in Roman times, the emperor) had a specialised network available. Philip Beale has recently written a history of both the official and unofficial postal network, and traces the modern amalgamated service to 1635, when the King's Post was made available to the public (Beale 2005, 7).

STEAM ON THE ROAD: AN OPPORTUNITY LOST?

It is estimated that the number of horses used for transport had gradually risen during the nineteenth century, to reach a total of 1.7 million by 1901 (Barker 1993, 145). Though railways dominated long-distance journeys, both passenger and freight, the horse was still in increasing demand for local journeys, and for feeder routes to link with the railway network. There were few competitors on the roads. In towns, passenger services were mostly horse-drawn, with hackneys and carriages for hire, supplemented in some towns by trams and omnibuses. Electric trams were starting to appear, by the end of the century, in London and some other large towns, though horse-drawn trams and omnibuses were still growing in popularity. For heavy freight haulage, horses were also still dominant; steam traction engines had begun to operate from the middle of the century, but by 1900 there were still only 8000 in use on the roads of England and Wales. By the 1890s, the first petrol-driven vehicles had started to appear, but these were still largely experimental and played no significant role in the transport system.

Considering the success of steam-power on the railways during the nineteenth century, it might seem surprising that steam did not play a greater role in road transport during that time. After all, the first three powered vehicles in the world were designed for road, not rail operation (McGowan 2004, 47ff). Precedence must go to Nicholas Cugnot, a French artillery officer who, in 1769, built a steam wagon for military purposes. Though it worked at slow speed, its boiler was inadequate to maintain sufficient pressure, and it was discontinued. It was another 30 years before a Cornishman, Richard Trevithick, built and tested two road vehicles. By the beginning of the nineteenth century he had already achieved a remarkable feat by building and selling steam engines powered by high-pressure boilers; these could provide at least half the power of the existing, massive, atmospheric engines, but were small enough to be moved from place to place by wagons pulled by horses. It was an obvious next step to see whether a steam engine could propel itself.

First, however, unaware of Cugnot's work, Trevithick needed to conduct a simple, but vital experiment. In an age when every cart, wagon or carriage was hauled along by horses, its wheels turning passively, it was not obvious what would happen if power was applied directly to them. Would the wheels grip the road and drive the vehicle forward, or would they simply spin round, slipping on the road surface? Accordingly Trevithick and his confidant, Davies Gilbert, parked a wagon on a slope, disconnected the horses, and then pressed down on the spokes to see if they could make the wagon move uphill. This they succeeded in doing, and, thus reassured, Trevithick put in hand work which has led, one way and another, to every self-powered vehicle on road or rail, ever since.

The experiment probably took place in 1800; the following year, Trevithick demonstrated his first road vehicle, called the 'Cambourne Flyer' near Cambourne in Cornwall. It travelled at more than walking speed on its first outing, before being destroyed by fire because Trevithick and his partner had forgotten to damp down the furnace when they left the vehicle to have a celebration lunch. The second, demonstrated in London in 1803, also operated successfully. It was well received by most onlookers, though it was pelted with cabbages by operators of horse-drawn hackneys, who saw it as competition. Though the vehicle worked well enough, Trevithick was worried that the uneven surfaces of the streets would damage any vehicle attempting to travel at a reasonable speed. He judged that rail-mounted locomotives offered a better prospect and in 1804 built the first railway locomotive in the world, drawing wagons along an iron railway which had previously been operated by horse-power, between the Pen-y-darren Iron Works and the Glamorganshire Canal, in South Wales. Though Trevithick soon lost interest in locomotion, all future steam-powered vehicles, whether for rail or road operation, depended on his invention of the high-pressure boiler; without it, the power-to-weight ratio would have been impossibly small. From then on, most technical efforts and investment went into rail operation; low friction between the iron rails and wheels offered the prospect of efficient freight operation, and, somewhat as an after-thought, passenger travel as well.

But it was probably the prospect of passenger travel, in competition with the expanding stage-coach market, which spurred on the few designers who took up the challenge of building a steam-powered road vehicle (Bird 1969, 174ff). These included Walter Hancock, who invented an improved boiler in 1826, and for the next 40 years produced and operated a series of steam carriages, many of which operated regular services. He, like many of his colleagues, struggled with finance, and an uneasy relationship with the railway companies; he was still persisting when the notorious Red Flag Act of 1865 killed off the entire market for steam-powered passenger vehicles on the road. Traction engines, hauling heavy loads, could still operate economically at the walking pace demanded by the Act, but it was speed, not raw power, which the passenger vehicles offered. Had there been a strong enough demand for fast road vehicles in the mid-nineteenth century, no doubt the Act could not have been passed; but railway and horse-power interests were strong enough to ensure that the full potential of such vehicles was never properly demonstrated. The repeal of the Act, 30 years later, sparked a revival of interest in steam on the road, but by then the internal combustion engine had begun its inexorable rise, eclipsing steam at the very moment it could have become the dominant power source for road vehicles.

THE EARLY TWENTIETH CENTURY: THE MOTOR CAR WINS, BUT THE HORSE STILL COMES IN SECOND

It could be argued that the Red Flag Act was poorly drafted; it failed to make the speed limit flexible, so that vehicles below a certain weight could travel at a higher speed; this effectively eliminated any incentive to develop lighter, cheaper and more manoeuvrable steam vehicles (Bird 1969, 194). It was 30 years later that this provision came in, probably at the behest of the early motor vehicle industry; linking speed limit to vehicle weight has been a cornerstone of legislation covering road vehicles ever since.

Besides introducing the notion of a speed limit linked to weight, several Acts of Parliament and Orders between 1896 and 1904 established the rather arcane

Licensed Vehicles in Great Britain, 1900-1940

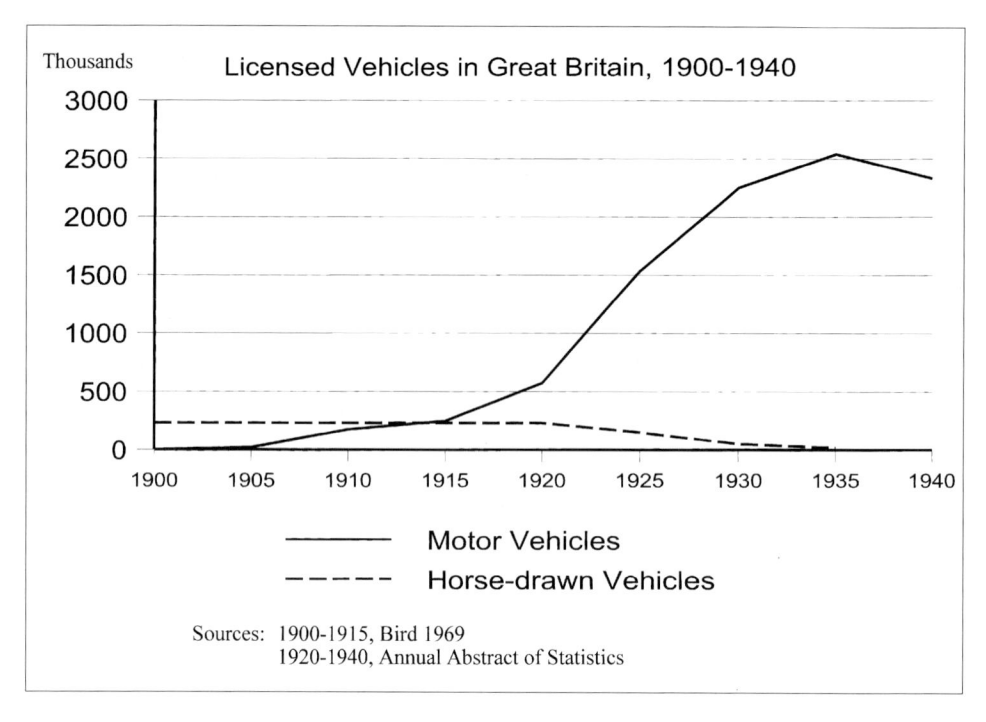

Sources: 1900-1915, Bird 1969
1920-1940, Annual Abstract of Statistics

66 The number of horse-drawn and motor vehicle licences issued between 1900 and 1940

definitions used to this day; vehicles operating under normal licensing are either motor cars or heavy motor cars; we would recognise these as cars and light vans on the one hand, or lorries and buses on the other. These early Acts covering motor vehicles set up the system of licensing for both vehicles and drivers; horse-drawn vehicles also needed licences, so we can piece together a reasonable, though far from comprehensive, picture of vehicles on the road during the first four decades of the twentieth century (66).

In the early years, horse-drawn vehicles predominated, with over 200,000 licensed vehicles, for goods and passenger use, together with about 10,000 steam vehicles and a few dozen petrol-driven cars. But it was amongst the latter that the growth was occurring, steadily at first, but rapidly accelerating after the First World War. Huge numbers of motor vehicles were decommissioned from military use, and their numbers were soon supplemented by new peace-time output from manufacturers. Numbers rose to over 0.5 million by 1920 and accelerated up to 2.5 million by 1940. The roads soon proved inadequate to deal with this influx, both in terms of wear and congestion. However, only a few bypasses were actually built before the outbreak of the Second World War, together with rebuilding of some of the London arterials, such as the Great West Road and Western Avenue. These developments seem to have been greeted with the same dismay and opposition by those who lived along the roads as occurs today (see below 'Attitudes to traffic').

Weight limit legislation in the 1930s quickly made steam vehicles uneconomic, but, notwithstanding the rapid rise of motor vehicle licences, horse-drawn ones did not fade out immediately, with 18,796 licences still in operation in 1935 (Statistical Abstracts of the United Kingdom, 80, 1937). Even as cars and lorries, powered by internal combustion engines, were flooding the roads, horse-drawn vehicles faded only slowly: why?

No doubt sheer conservatism, even snobbery, played a part. Members of the gentry who had just acquired the wealth to aspire to a fine horse-drawn carriage from which to advertise their status, were not keen to use these upstart vehicles; they looked askance at their owners, who seemed to be interested in the mechanics of their vehicles, and were keen to *drive*, rather than sit in the back (Bird 1969, 211).

But snobbery was not the only reason why horse-power was slow to decline; there were economic arguments too. Two examples illustrate the view of those who needed to look to their profits: the first concerns Sainsbury's. Though by the 1920s they had started using light motor vans for deliveries within 12-15 miles (18-23km) of the firm's headquarters, the vehicles were, until then, too slow for longer trips. For these journeys, goods were crated, taken by horse-drawn wagons to the nearest rail siding, transported by rail, and the process reversed via a siding as near as possible to the destination premises. It was not until 1937 that the firm parted with its last horse (Barker 1993, 190). The second example concerns the heavy haulage firm Wynns. Founded in 1863, its first power source was the horse, and, as it turned out, it was the last but one, only being phased out in the late 1930s, with steam having come and gone in the meantime. In 1890, heavy trailers were available which could handle 40-ton loads, but each of these was still being hauled by horses, a team of 48, four abreast, being harnessed up for this purpose. Steam traction engines, such as those made by Fowlers, were introduced in the 1890s, but phased out again in the early 1920s, being replaced by more modern Foden and Sentinel steam lorries. But these had also gone by the early 1930s – made uneconomic by axle load legislation – while horses were still in use, for example, to haul tipper wagons during the construction of Western Avenue, in Cardiff, in the late 1930s (Wynn 2003, 5).

THE RISE AND RISE OF THE MOTOR CAR

As we have seen there was a rapid rise of motor vehicle licences during the 1920s and '30s. Although this brought with it the realisation that the existing

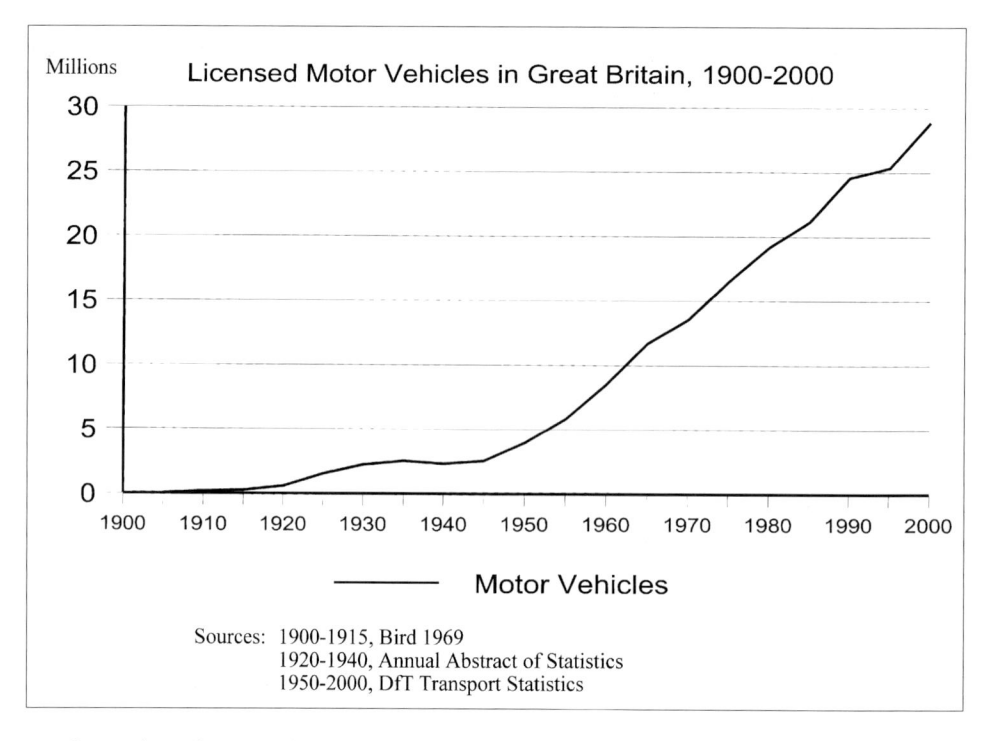

Licensed Motor Vehicles in Great Britain, 1900-2000

Sources: 1900-1915, Bird 1969
1920-1940, Annual Abstract of Statistics
1950-2000, DfT Transport Statistics

67 The number of motor vehicle licences issued between 1900 and 2000

road network needed to be developed, there could have been little expectation of what was to follow (67). The figure shows the number of motor vehicles licensed each year throughout the twentieth century (note that the scale is now millions, rather than thousands as in the previous figure). With a slight decline because of the Second World War, and its economic aftermath, vehicle numbers have increased, year by year, at an even faster rate than before. Over 80 per cent of the more than 30 million vehicles on the road are private cars, so the twentieth century saw an unprecedented level of access to individually controlled transport provision. Horses, either to ride or to pull one's own carriage, never provided such opportunities for other than a tiny minority of the population. Only walking and, towards the end of the nineteenth century, cycling can claim to have been, historically, more accessible modes of individual transport. As far as travel as a passenger is concerned, there have, of course, from Roman times onwards, been opportunities to travel on freight carts or wagons as a passenger. However it was not until the late seventeenth century that specialist services for carrying passengers began to appear, and it was not until the stage-coach era of the early nineteenth century that long journeys as a passenger were at all comfortable, reliable and convenient. The railways gave a huge boost to public transport opportunities during the latter half of that century, and, perhaps, gave people a taste for fast travel by land. Though many journeys are still made by other modes, the private car is now a major source of passenger journeys, in addition to those made by drivers themselves.

THE HEY-DAY OF THE BICYCLE

Though cycling is currently becoming more popular, it still represents less than 2 per cent of total distance travelled by cars (DfT Transport Statistics Table 9.7). Yet 70 years ago there were as many bicycles on the roads as cars, and the distance they travelled was comparable. Cycling was nearing the end of its heyday; from then on cars became more numerous and travelled further, while cycling suffered a continuous decline, which is only now being reversed.

From 1870 the 'boneshaker' with its wooden wheels and iron tyres began to appear on Britain's roads, shortly followed by the 'Penny-farthing'; this latter machine with its very large front wheel, was able to travel along rough roads with less effort. By about 1890 most of the elements of the modern machine had been introduced: geared pedals, wheels of equal diameter with metal spokes and rims, pneumatic tyres etc. (Higman 2002). Cyclists began to enjoy newfound freedom; a cyclist could cover as much ground in a day as a horse-rider, and cycling, for both recreation and ordinary journey-making, became popular, and even a passion, for both men and women.

These new road users were far from welcomed by horse-riders and drivers of wagons and carriages, and in 1887 the Cycling Touring Club was established to represent their interests. Cyclists were hardly more popular with the newly emerging motor vehicle drivers, but they held their own with the newcomers, both in terms of numbers and distance travelled, until well into the 1930s.

Road-builders at first ignored cyclists altogether, and were later criticised for not providing adequate width for cycle paths (Bressey and Lutyens 1938, 24). In response to such pressures, a Ministry of Transport circular of March 1936 required that footways and cycle paths be placed alongside major new roads. By contrast, the post-Second World War motorways specifically exclude both cyclists and pedestrians, the space formerly devoted to these facilities being taken by the hard shoulders alongside traffic lanes.

Modern facilities for cyclists, such as cycle lanes and special crossing lights, are rather patchy in implementation, but outside towns there are many opportunities available (68). The most recent development has been the achievement of 10,000 miles (15,000km) of the National Cycle Network, a series of linked cycle and pedestrian routes, designed to join up traffic-calmed areas with ordinary roads

68 Cyclists on the public right of way, which follows the preserved line of the Roman road called the Devil's Highway, near Crowthorne, Berkshire

which have low levels of traffic, using dedicated paths. The latter often use dismantled railway lines; it was one of the these, between Bristol and Bath, which, in 1977, was the first to be converted. The network was originally conceived, and has since been designed and promoted, by a consultancy called SUSTRANS (SUStainable TRANSport) (*69*).

THE JUGGERNAUT COMETH

There are numerous categories of vehicle on the roads, other than the private car, such as the light van, taxi, bus, minibus, motorcycle and bicycle, but none of these has as much impact as the heavy lorry. The fact that it is colloquially known as the 'juggernaut' gives a clue to its often unwelcome presence on the nation's roads, and

69 Opening of the first section of the National Cycle Network in 1984. This stretch follows the abandoned line of the old Bristol–Bath railway, and now carries over two million trips per year. Courtesy SUSTRANS; www.sustrans.org.uk

many people have protested about the size, noise and apparent danger posed by such vehicles. On the other hand, the role of heavy lorries can easily be defended on the ground that it provides a vital mode of transport for the movement of freight. The relative merits of the economic and environmental cases for and against the lorry are beyond the scope of this book. However, the history of the lorry is inextricably linked to the history of road design, so it is worth considering as a special case.

We have already looked at how roads have been made thicker and stronger to enable them to cope with repeated applications of heavy wheel loads (see Chapter 4), but to avoid the need to build totally uneconomic road structures, some other measures have proved necessary to lessen the impact of the lorry. In this section we shall see how vehicle design (and legislation to control it) have together achieved the neat trick of allowing lorries to get much heavier without imposing an unacceptable burden on the road.

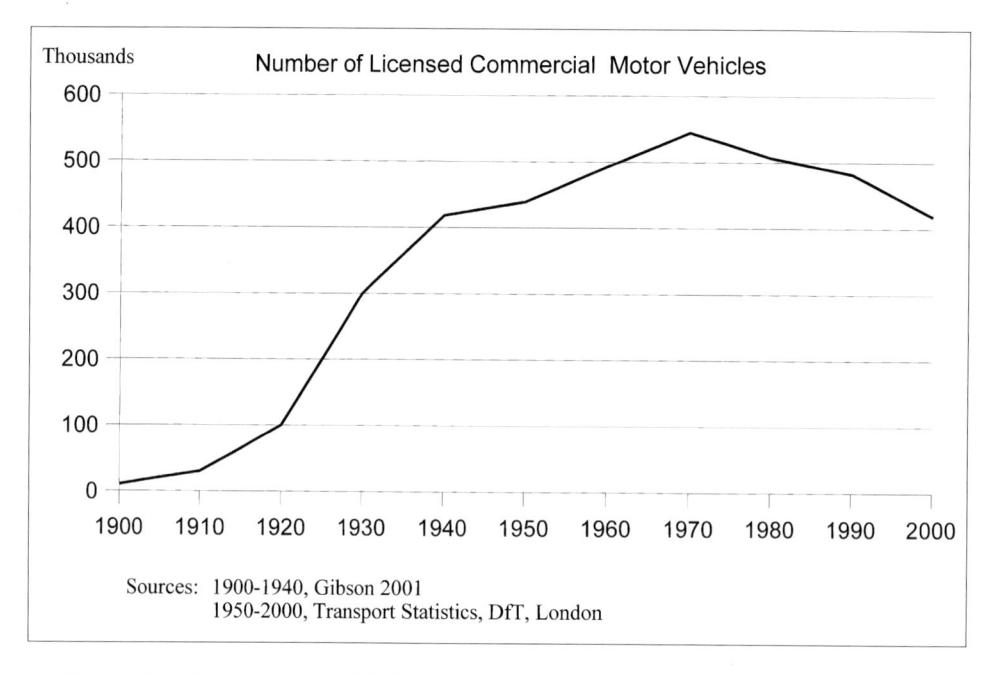

FROM TRACKWAYS TO MOTORWAYS: 5000 YEARS OF HIGHWAY HISTORY

Number of Licensed Commercial Motor Vehicles

Sources: 1900-1940, Gibson 2001
1950-2000, Transport Statistics, DfT, London

70 The number of commercial vehicle licences issued between 1900 and 2000

The sheer visual impact of lorries has led many to assume that their numbers must be increasing, along with cars. Although the number of light vans is still rising, when it comes to lorries (known as Goods Vehicles in the statistics) there is rather a different picture (*70*).

Although the number of Goods Vehicles increased until the 1960s, in much the same manner as did the total of licensed vehicles, this reached a peak in 1968, at just under 600,000, and thereafter has shown a slow decline. The most likely reason for this decline is the increase in allowable lorry weight which has occurred. Before we look at how lorry weights have changed it is worth noting the long and complicated history of such an apparently simple concept.

Awareness that heavy wheeled vehicles can cause damage to roads, together with official attempts to limit vehicle weights, date back to Roman times (see Appendix). But it does not appear in English legislation until a proclamation of James I limited wagons to 1 ton in weight (though without specifying a means for checking whether this weight had been exceeded) (Pawson 1977, 219). In 1662 the load that could be carried (thus excluding the weight of the wagon) was 2 tons in summer, less in winter. However, until 1741 there was no provision for weighing wagons; after this, Turnpike Trustees had authority to erect suitable machinery, though how many did so is not recorded. By 1773 there was an upper limit of 8 tons, though below this there had gradually grown up an extremely complex system of limits, according to which the wider the wheels and the farther apart they were on the wagon the greater the permitted limit. Later Acts also included limits on the number of horses pulling a wagon, presumably on the grounds that the more horses there were, the heavier the vehicle was likely to be.

Width of wheels was still considered important as Steam Traction Engines began to use the roads; in 1878 a weight limit was imposed which increased by 1 ton for every additional inch width of wheel, with an upper limit of 14 tons. During the 1890s, the Red Flag Act was effectively lifted for vehicles which had an unladen weight of no more than 3 tons.

Up to this time, all mechanically propelled vehicles were described as locomotives, but in 1904 the term 'Motor Car' and 'Heavy Motor Car' were introduced to relate to the newly appearing light vehicles (Armstrong *et al.* 2003, 421, 427). Though the lower limit, defined by unladen weight, has remained the same, the upper one, using gross weight, has increased dramatically, with different limits depending on the number of axles (*71*). Note that limits were metricated in 1973; thus the figure shows the limits in imperial tons before this date and metric tonnes (t) afterwards (the difference between the two is minimal; 1 ton equals 1.017 tonnes).

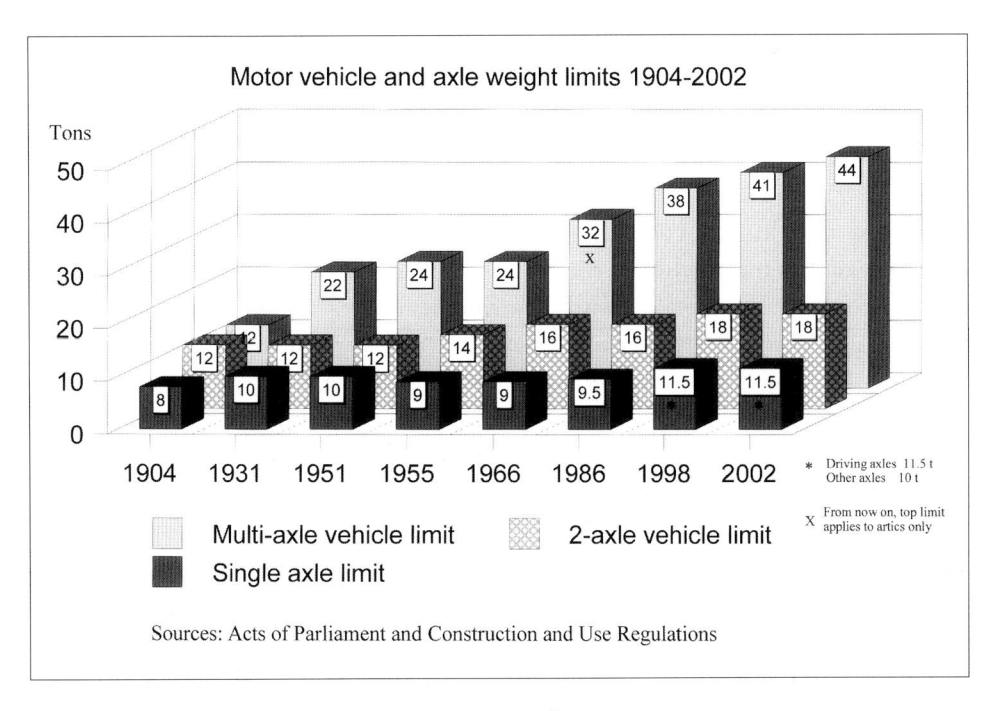

71 Commercial vehicle weight limits, between 1900 and 2000

In 1904, when all vehicles had two axles only, the gross limit was set at 12 tons. The two-axle vehicle limit has since risen by only 50 per cent, now standing at 18t. By contrast, the absolute upper limit has been allowed to rise by a factor of over three and a half, from 12 tons to 44t, with the required number of axles rising from two to six. Before 1966 the heaviest lorries could be four-axle rigid vehicles, but since that date, with the required number of axles for the top limit rising, first to five, and later to six, the heaviest lorries have had to operate with a trailer, either as part of an articulated vehicle or towed behind a rigid goods carrier.

We saw in Chapter 4 that the wear on roads increases as the fourth power of the weight of a wheel passing over it. It has proved possible to build roads strong enough to carry axles of about 10 tons weight; by increasing the number of axles, while keeping a strict limit on the maximum load to be carried by each one, 44t lorries can be made to cause no more damage than if the load was distributed among a number of two-axle vehicles, each subject to the same maximum axle load. Modern lorries also have to conform to complex requirements for axle spacing and suspension, both of which are needed to ensure that the impact on the road is minimised.

Much heavier loads can be carried, but only under stringent additional conditions, which often means notifying highway authorities, the Highways Agency, Police and perhaps central government as well, to ensure that damage to roads and bridges, and disruption to traffic, are minimised. Even when loads of several hundred tonnes are being moved, axle loads are kept under strict control; for example, a load comprising a 250t power-station component, and carried on a trailer which itself might weight over 100t, would be supported on a set of bogies comprising a total of at least 18 axles.

DANGER ON THE ROADS

Introduction
'Road safety' is a well-developed branch of knowledge; making roads safer is a major objective of government policy, and much of the legislation covering vehicles and drivers is aimed at achieving this objective. It can of course be argued that the term Road Safety is a euphemism: what we really mean is 'road danger'. The roads are not, and never have been, *safe* in the absolute sense. As shown below, the nature of the dangers faced by road users has altered during our history, but the attitude of travellers to them seems fairly consistent; namely that people are aware that there are potential hazards confronting them on the road, but are hardly ever deterred, by this knowledge, from making journeys. In this section we shall look at how road safety became an issue in the first few

decades of the motor era, but first we look at the problems encountered by travellers in earlier eras.

Hazards on the road before the motor age

It is the speed and volume of traffic which causes the main hazards to road users in the motor age, for both pedestrians and vehicle occupants (see next sub-section). However, for most of our history, road users faced very different hazards. Though an approaching group of horseman or a stage-coach pulled by six horses could seem pretty intimidating, the sheer noise and commotion of their approach, and the fact that they were probably travelling at no more than 10-12mph meant that there was time for other road users to get out of their way. While the chances of being run over or collided with may have been less than they are today, there were other hazards to contend with which we do not worry too much about nowadays.

Perhaps the most important of these hazards was linked to the weather; a contemporary report of 1406 lists numerous impassable roads, along with numerous bridges in danger of collapse (Bland 1957, 6). Away from towns there may have been no bridges at all to cross rivers or streams. There could be real dangers when using fords or ferries, especially when the water was swollen following wet weather; in Chapter 4 we saw that Abingdon Bridge was built following the drowning of several people while attempting to cross the Thames by ferry. We have also already encountered John Metcalf (Blind Jack); he gained a reputation for rescuing people from drowning as they attempted to make such crossings. We have also referred to the chaise of John Metcalf's friend Colonel Liddell being slowed to below average walking speed by rain on the road, despite the availability of numerous servants accompanying the vehicle to help get it out of trouble. Even on horseback, the weather needed to be respected. We can see examples of this in the progress of a group of regular business travellers, the Warden and Fellows of Merton College Oxford (Martin 1975). Detailed records have survived of their travels during the fourteenth and fifteenth centuries to the College's various properties all over England. They travelled at all times of year, staying overnight in modest accommodation. On one such journey, in 1461, the sub-Warden, Richard de Scardeburgh, travelled to Canterbury; while there he was delayed for a day because of rain, while on the way back, at Wycombe he waited another day because of 'distemper of the air', which Martin interprets as probably fog. On a later journey he was delayed because his horse became ill, possibly as a consequence of him having travelled 40 miles (64km) the previous day, a long distance on a winter day.

Political disturbances and riots were frequent in the Middle Ages; the Merton College officials were certainly delayed by these on occasions. For the most part such disturbances were not directly connected to roads or transport, though there was a period, during the turnpike era of the eighteenth century, when resentment at the necessity of paying tolls led to disturbances on the road itself. For example, colliers destroyed gates in Bristol in 1724, and by 1735 so widespread had violent opposition to tolls become that the government made damage to such property a capital offence (Albert 1979).

More common than being caught up in a riot was the risk of personal attack. We have already encountered, in Chapter 2, the King's Peace, which was supposed to deter robbers from preying on people on the principal roads. It is not at all clear whether such measures had any practical effect, but it seems likely that travellers would normally need to take their own precautions. Besides common robbers, including the famous highwaymen, there could also be threats from more high-born villains. J.J. Jusserand recounts an event which took place in 1342, when some merchants petitioned the Earl of Arundel for redress because their servants, carrying valuable spices to market at Stafford, had been robbed by Sir Robert Rideware and his men. One of the servants escaped and raised the alarm at Lichfield. Though the King's bailiff's men had recovered the spices, they themselves were set upon by the robbers and the spices stolen once more (Jusserand 1889, 74).

There was also a real risk of a carriage being overturned. In November 1762, Boswell travelled in a chaise from Edinburgh to London, and suffered this fate between Stamford and Stilton, when a horse bolted, giving both him and the driver 'a pretty severe rap'. On the same journey he also suffered a broken wheel and the worry of imminent robbery when they arrived at Biggleswade, well after dark (Morley 1961, 234). Yet Boswell's initial elation at the prospect of his journey does not seem to have been dimmed by what happened during it. It is also interesting to compare Boswell's journey, much of which was along the Great North Road, with that of Metcalf and Liddell along the same route from London to Harrogate. In 1748 the latter travelled at about 35 miles per day, less than 25 years later, the former at over 80.

Nowadays we do not tend to worry much about the weather, riots or robbery. However, these hazards have been replaced by a new one, namely the risk of collision with other road users. We can track this process by using statistics on road casualties which have been compiled from 1875 onwards, a year which just predates the first appearance of motor vehicles.

Road safety in the motor age
For most of our history there are no sources of information to tell us how many people were killed or injured on Britain's roads. This changed from the mid-nineteenth century; roads and what happened on them began to become the

USING THE ROADS

responsibility, first of local government above parish level, and then of central government. Along with this change of responsibility came the collection of data on road casualties, showing how many people were killed or injured in any given year. Nowadays we tend to group fatalities and serious injuries together under the heading KSI (killed or seriously injured), along with another category, total casualties, which also includes the much larger number of those who are injured less seriously. However, it is the annual number of fatalities which has been collected for the longest period, and therefore allows us to give road casualties a historical context; accordingly these are used throughout in the following analysis (72).

The graph shows approximately how many people were killed on Britain's roads from 1875 to 2002. For the first 35 years, fatalities remained fairly constant, at around 1500, while by 2002 they had risen to nearly 3500. But the period in between shows some dramatic changes, which illustrate the impact of the rapid rise and present-day dominance of the motor vehicle.

A detailed breakdown of the first year's figures shows that two-thirds of fatalities involved carts or wagons, as distinct from horse-drawn omnibuses, trams and carriages, or individual horses. Thus vehicles carrying goods rather than

Annual fatalities on the roads of Great Britain since 1875

Sources: 1900-1910, Road Accident Statistics 1986, 16 (England and Wales only)
1910-1945, Annual Abstract of Statistics
1950-2002, Department of Transport, Road Accident Data, 2004, Table 9.10.

72 Annual number of fatalities on the roads of Great Britain between 1870 and 2000

passengers were the main hazard. Unfortunately it is not clear which category of road user suffered these fatalities, though it would be reasonable to assume a substantial proportion were pedestrians because they were the most common road user; the cost of owning or hiring a horse, or travelling in a vehicle was too expensive for most people.

By the time we reach 1910, although the total fatalities were similar to those that occurred over 30 years earlier, a third now involved some sort of powered vehicle, such as cars, vans, cabs and motorcycles. Steam-powered vehicles accounted for very few deaths in 1910, amongst which were 23 involving traction engines and two from steam rollers. Only one type of powered vehicle competed with horse-drawn carts and wagons as a cause of fatalities, namely the motor car; thus the main hazard on the modern road had begun to make an impact even then, though it would have been hard to predict what was to come.

We saw earlier (66, 67) how rapidly the number of motor vehicles rose during the twentieth century; the effect of this rise is a major factor in the history of road accidents. It can be seen from figure 72 that, in parallel with that of vehicles, the number of road deaths also began to rise rapidly after about 1910, with no real sign of levelling off until the early 1930s. Alarm about the rising toll on the road had led to the introduction of such measures as the 30mph speed limit in built-up areas, pedestrian crossings and improved driver training. All this was put at nought very quickly in the early years of the Second World War, when road deaths reached over 8000 per year, a figure not seen before or since. It seems probable that, while petrol was still available, people could continue to drive, but the blackout made night driving hazardous. Severe shortages of fuel soon cut the amount of traffic, and road deaths fell substantially from 1942 onwards. However, when people were able to drive again, traffic resumed its previous rise, and so did road casualties, with annual fatalities increasing from 5000 per year in 1950 to a peak of 7,763 in 1972.

Though the rise is neither so steep or extensive as between 1910 and 1930, the overall figure disguises a dramatic new element. While pedestrians, cyclists and motorcycle riders had long been the most vulnerable road users, vehicle occupants had seemed comparatively safe. In 1950, when total fatalities stood at 5012, only 827 involved vehicle occupants, car drivers or passengers, amounting to 15 per cent of the total; by 1972 the total had risen by 50 per cent, but deaths among vehicle occupants rose four times as fast, reaching over 3500, nearly half the total.

It was perhaps this element of the casualty figures which led to the introduction of now familiar measures such as compulsory seat-belt wearing and maximum limits on blood alcohol levels for drivers. More recently better road and vehicle design, the introduction of traffic calming, deployment of speed cameras and better awareness of safety among road users has seen a steady reduction in fatalities.

All this has been achieved despite a continuing rise in the number of vehicles on the road; clearly something significant is happening to the *rate* at which casualties are occurring per vehicle. Looking again at figure 72, we can see that in 1924 the annual fatality level was about the same as in 2000. Though the number of motor vehicles was increasing rapidly, it had, as we noted above, still only reached 1 million. With total vehicles at just under 30 million in 2000, it is clear that *per vehicle* the roads are 30 times safer. This is a substantial achievement, but the continuing rise in vehicles, and the distances they are driven, means that there needs to be continuing improvement in road safety measures to maintain this trend. We still have some way to go before we can improve on the fatality level evident in an era when the fastest entity on the roads was a galloping horse; we can have our freedom to own cars and drive them when and where we choose, but unless we can accept some continuing restriction on our freedom in the interests of safety, we may never get back to that early fatality level, let alone improve upon it.

ATTITUDES TO TRAFFIC

The relentless rise of traffic, both in the volume and size of vehicles, has altered the lives of those living near our main roads. While the population at large benefits from greater mobility and reduced transport costs, those who live near main roads suffer a significant disadvantage; noise, fumes and danger are measurable, but less obvious is the feeling of being cut off from one's neighbours by a busy road, a phenomenon known as *severance*. Efforts are of course made to mitigate these effects, both by physical alterations to the environment and the design of vehicles, but the feeling is widespread that living near a busy road is wholly unwelcome, and to be avoided if at all possible. Yet, our attitudes to roads are not that simple; people can feel ambivalent, or even nostalgic about the road they live by, while at the same time feeling angry and worried about what it is like now. These feelings come into focus when a new road development scheme is proposed; two examples are given below of developments which have occurred on the A40 trunk road, which for centuries has been a principal artery out of London, carrying traffic to Oxford, Gloucester and onward to Fishguard Harbour and other destinations in South Wales.

In 1921 a proposal was made to bypass Uxbridge, west London; it was decided to take the new road to the north, through greenfield areas, thus avoiding the need to demolish houses. After some delay, and objections to the loss of some allotments, the bypass was opened in 1928, to be called Western Avenue. This event was greeted with great press acclaim, though many local residents were still unhappy, particularly as they had to cross the new road on a footbridge. Despite such misgivings, the road soon attracted new housing, shops and light industrial construction, including the famous Hoover Building. These newcomers seemed to relish the prospect of living and working next to this and other new arterial roads; what became known as 'ribbon development' spread rapidly. The phenomenon soon caused official worries, on the grounds that the countryside was being spoiled, culminating in the Development Act of 1935, but by this time, Western Avenue had acquired an almost continuous row of buildings along it. The character of much of the housing, comprising semi-detached dwellings with mock-Tudor styling, was criticised by satirists such as Osbert Lancaster, who coined the phrase 'bypass variegated' to describe it. This suggests that people were happy to embrace the new transport environment, with its prospect of car-ownership for all, while at the same time rejecting the modern movement of architects such as le Corbusier.

At a point which had been the focus of the 1920s protests, a major junction had been established, known as Gipsy Corner, and in the early 1990s it was proposed that many of the houses lining the road needed to be demolished to allow a major expansion of this junction's capacity. The reaction of the people living near Gipsy Corner, the consultation exercise and the commencement of the work itself, is recounted in a charming and evocative book by Edward Platt, who also provided the historic background to Western Avenue outlined above (Platt 2001). The book comprises a series of interviews with the local residents. Many of them had lived next to, or near, Western Avenue since childhood, and had fond memories of what the road was like 20 or 30 years earlier, when it was 'quiet'. One of the interviewees recalled her childhood excitement of living by the road to Oxford, a town she had not visited but which loomed large and romantically in her imagination. Everyone seemed to feel that there should be an alternative to further expansion of the road; but, given that the work was going ahead, some were happy enough to move away, while others clung on to the last possible moment before being compulsorily re-housed.

A similar pattern of development had already taken place further west along the same road. During the 1930s a bypass had been built to carry the A40 trunk road north of Oxford which had, for centuries, passed through the crowded city centre. Though, as in the previous example, the bypass was built largely over green fields, urban expansion soon filled the intervening space between the new road and the city itself, with the development of suburbs such as Summertown and Sunnymead. To these new residents this was not a bypass at all, but part of their local environment. Thus, in the 1960s, when proposals were laid for a major upgrade of the road to cope with the rising volumes of traffic, there were strong objections; far from making provision for even more traffic, the local people pressed for a new bypass, further north still, to link with the proposed new M40 motorway. The campaigners lost their case, and the road through Sunnymead was expanded to dual carriageway status, with major junctions to give access to service roads (Herbert 1971).

Both these examples demonstrate our ambivalence to roads. When a new one is built to take traffic away from people who have long complained about it, housing and other development seems to follow the new road, as if a new set of people relish the excitement, activity and opportunities of living near it. As traffic grows yet further, and these newcomers get older, their attitude changes; they in turn want the traffic to be taken elsewhere. If instead, there is a proposal to upgrade the road, to give it the capacity it clearly now needs, they are opposed, seeing it as confirmation that the road is set to carry even more traffic in the future. Building new roads to take traffic away from where people live is a difficult task in any case; it becomes self-defeating if people then proceed to take up residence along them.

7

CONCLUSIONS AND SPECULATIONS

In this book I have tried to put Britain's roads centre stage. This is not because roads lack a public or political profile; quite the opposite in fact, with arguments raging about matters like the use of tolls, speed cameras, and whether new roads generate more traffic. Taking a long, historical perspective, while interesting in its own right, can help to illuminate what is going on today. What I have tried to do is show how roads have been, and still are, the outcome of how we desire and choose to travel over land; clearly, once they are in place, roads give us a travel opportunity, but they would not be there at all if there had not already been a travel demand which needed to be met. This demand not only determines where roads go, but also their structure and shape. A separate consideration of these three factors, from the Roman period to the present day, forms the central part of the book, in Chapters 3, 4 and 5 respectively. In the prehistoric period, before the Romans arrived here, it is not really possible to distinguish these factors clearly, so Chapter 2 considers all aspects of road-building during the Mesolithic, Neolithic, Bronze and Iron Ages. We end, in Chapter 6, with a consideration of the road user. This may seem perverse; in light of the statement made above that roads are the outcome of the way they are used. But the trends of road use have been so profound and dramatic over the last 100 years that we need to highlight them if we are to look ahead. Finally, there is an Appendix containing a chronological list of significant dates in our road history.

The first evidence we have of journey-making comes from the Mesolithic period, over 6000 years ago, provided by the preserved footprints of people walking along the shoreline of some of our largest river estuaries. These were hunter-gatherers, moving from place to place in search of game and wild fruit and nuts. No doubt they had devised regular pathways through familiar areas, but there is no evidence of any kind of construction. With the advent of farming, in the Neolithic and Bronze Ages, we see definable settlements, such as South Hornchurch, Essex, and, by the same token, definable trackways, to serve them. Often these comprised droveways, narrow strips of land flanked by ditches, along which animals could be driven to pasture or, perhaps, to market. It is appropriate to be a little cautious about the latter as a destination, because it implies a 'market economy' for which there is little evidence. Exchange and barter were the more usual forms of transaction, so there may not have been identifiable centres where animals, or any other commodity for that matter, would be brought for sale. This has a consequence for what we would expect of the trackways; if there were markets, we might expect to find, if we're lucky, evidence of how people and their animals travelled to and from them. So far, droveways do not seem to connect up into anything resembling a network; they have only been found in or near definable settlements. Thus, if there is indeed a network waiting to be found, we have only located its nodes (or some of them), without the links between. Rather the opposite is the case with what might be described as the first application of road technology, namely the timber trackways, found in waterlogged areas, such as fens, levels and river estuaries. Examples such as Bramcote Green, Bermondsey, on the south shore of the Thames, show how these trackways were designed to enable people to walk, dry-shod, across such areas; the timbers gradually sank into the water and mud, being preserved until now. Very often, short lengths of these trackways have been found without direct evidence of where they were going. Thus, in contrast to droveways, we have the links without the nodes.

There is little evidence of bridges, or structures made of stone, so whatever provision was made for getting around would have been low-key in the extreme. But this should not be regarded as in any way primitive or inadequate. The system was fit-for-purpose, in a society which was largely rural and local; no doubt there were regular travellers, but their demand was insufficient to bring into existence anything resembling a connected network.

It is worth noting that this view would be hotly contested by those who believe that, at least as far back as the Neolithic, there was indeed a civilisation in Britain which needed long-distance travel, and whose members were capable of laying out a sophisticated set of roads to provide it. Enter the ley-hunters, who seek out linear alignments of landscape features, both natural and man-made, and conjure up the existence of straight tracks between them. There are also

CONCLUSIONS AND SPECULATIONS

advocates of long-distance surveying of great accuracy, who seek confirmation of their views in the apparent precision with which widely dispersed features are related. Often the flaw lies in the selective use of evidence; by doing this, it is remarkably easy to find such patterns and alignments, and to go on from there to create a theory on what is, in fact, no more than coincidence.

Perhaps we can have a little more sympathy with the rather larger group who see the Ridgeways as of prehistoric origin. Terms such as Britain's (or even Europe's) Oldest Road are happily used to describe the by-now well-preserved tracks which follow the watersheds of our chalk and limestone ridges. The fact that many of these seem to end up in the vicinity of Stonehenge lends apparent currency to the view that they were used by Neolithic folk to visit whatever ceremonies might have taken place there. In support, advocates of their great age point to the ancient sites, such as the Uffington White Horse, and Wayland's Smithy, which lie along them. But we now know that settlements were not confined to the high ground along these lines of hills, so that any tracks which linked them would be in the valleys too. When we look for direct evidence from excavation, the ridgeways do not seem to feature beneath Roman or post-Roman finds, and they do not appear on medieval documents such as the Gough Map. It seems most likely that a number of isolated paths were given prehistoric status, and then linked together in the imagination of Victorian antiquarians, who were seeking to demonstrate, much as the ley-hunters do, that there was an ancient and advanced civilisation here, long before the Romans.

As it happens, this search for a glorious and sophisticated past is not new. As far back as the medieval period, scholars were tracing the Four Royal Roads as having been built by a prehistoric British ruler. Maybe this was an attempt by the Anglo-Saxons to show that there was an even more powerful civilisation here long before the Normans arrived. A rather similar motive seems to lie behind a Celtic version of the same theme, in which Helen (or Elen) is supposed to have had roads built between fortresses in what is now Wales, which were named after her ' ... because men of the island would not have assembled for anyone else'. It is possible to see Helen as married to the short-lived Roman emperor Magnus Maximus. Thus, one would have hoped that we have a sustainable historical character to fall back on, but, unfortunately, the Celtic style is so steeped in a dreamlike storyline, that it is hard to get a firm grip on events.

As the Neolithic and Bronze Ages gave way to the Iron Age, new settlement types appeared, such as the hillforts and the nucleated form which the Romans called *oppida*. We can see the beginning of something resembling town streets, both at Danebury and Silchester, though often it is only possible to divine their location from the absence of anything else, such as buildings, pits, rubbish dumps etc. There is just a hint that levels of movement within these more concentrated areas was beginning to require some limited road-making, with evidence of the scattering of stones to make a layer of metalling. Perhaps this was a harbinger, albeit a quiet one, of what was to happen next.

I argue above that prehistoric tracks were fit-for-purpose in their time. With the arrival of the Romans, that purpose dramatically changed. When the Roman army arrived in Kent in the autumn of AD 43, they brought with them a wholly different social structure, which many among the various tribes of Britain were not long in adopting. There were three aspects of this new society which impacted on what sort of roads would be needed. Firstly, Roman society was an urban one, so there would soon be concentrated settlements needing supply and support; secondly, their thinking was strategic, not local, so that, whereas the Iron Age tribes operated at what we might now see as a county level, the new administration thought in terms of what we would now call regions, or even countries; and thirdly, transport was much more orientated towards wheeled vehicles, for both military and civilian movement of freight and supplies. The Roman road network, with its surveyed routes, direct alignments and well-engineered structures, was needed to fulfil this new purpose. Thus it should be seen, not as an arbitrarily imposed structure, designed to impress the locals and symbolise Roman power (though no doubt it did both of these), but to fulfil a predictable transport requirement.

Just as there was a very specific purpose to cause the Roman road network to be created, when the legions left nearly four centuries later, that purpose went too. Urban society seems to have rapidly declined, the focus became more local once more and wheeled traffic declined or disappeared altogether. High-quality roads were not needed, but of course such features do not disappear. So well made were Roman roads, with their metalling, ditches and raised *aggers*, that many just stayed in the landscape (and often still do), being used or ignored as the need arose. It was perhaps another 400 years before towns began to appear once more, and the need for a road network began to appear with them. Sometimes these towns were built on the sites of Roman ones, so the roads which went there could be reused. But others grew up elsewhere, requiring newly trodden tracks to serve them. A process of modifying the Roman network began, which, if we follow roads as marked on the Gough Map of 1350, had already led to a new network, part Roman, part post-Roman, which largely resembles our current network.

But these roads were pretty poor specimens compared to Roman ones, probably for the simple reason that they were not being required to carry heavy wheeled traffic. Between towns, they were often no more than wide, muddy spaces, through which travellers picked their way, looking for a comparatively dry path. This often necessitated moving out to the side, making the area even wider. In towns, travellers were confined to a narrow strip between buildings, so the street could be worn into a hollow, as shown at St George's Street, Canterbury. When, eventually, some metalling was spread, it failed to correct the hollow shape.

Rather more attention was paid to bridges, and some impressive structures were erected. The Thames had a large number of bridges by the thirteenth century; many survived for several hundred years, before being replaced, while others, such as Abingdon, still incorporate parts of the original structure. Even so, travellers could find their way blocked because a bridge had fallen down due to neglect.

Wheeled traffic did not reappear to any significant extent until the seventeenth century, at which point the roads were found to be ill-adapted to the greatly increased wear to which they were subjected. It took a new way of finance, with the turnpike tolls replacing the old parish-based system, and the development of good road structures and drainage, before road-building gradually caught up. Eventually, in the early nineteenth century, wheeled vehicles could travel without hindrance across Britain.

A critical factor was the discovery of the importance of carefully selecting stones to be used for metalling, though there was disagreement about what size of stone should be used. Telford advocated massive structures, with large stones forming a rigid foundation; McAdam, by contrast, determined that large stones were positively harmful, and should be dug up and broken into small pieces, before being placed back on the road. However, all agreed that, provided good-quality stone was used, the hard, unsprung wheels of heavy wagons would break up small surface stones even more, eventually compressing everything into a compact, waterproof surface. Though Telford's roads were undoubtedly successful, McAdam's were lighter, and therefore cheaper, so it was the latter's style which became immortalised in the term *macadamised* as a description of any smooth, but unbound surface.

Though macadamised roads were a huge advantage over the earlier ones, there were problems with an essentially open surface; it was dusty in summer and muddy in winter. During the rest of the nineteenth century, efforts were made to use natural asphalt, concrete, wood, cobbles, flagstones and various other materials to form robust surfaces. This all took some time; eventually the technique was developed of mixing basic ingredients, such as bitumen, sand and aggregate together, to form a spreadable surface material. Fortunately, this new approach was available in time for the motor age; just as well, because pneumatic tyres destroy, rather than enhance, macadamised roads. However, so closely was McAdam's name associated with road-making, that the new, chemically bound surface was called *tarmacadam* (or just *tarmac*), despite the fact that the man himself had never advocated, or even experimented with, such an approach.

It was one thing to have a basic technique available, quite another to realise how quickly roads would be overwhelmed in the early twentieth century; roads again found themselves under pressure as the motor vehicle began its rise. It took several decades of the motor age to learn how to deal with the much heavier vehicles which the new form of propulsion produced.

Looking back, it is clear that, for most of our history, where problems have arisen, it has been because of inadequate road strength; wheels are more demanding than feet or hooves, while heavily laden wheels are dramatically more demanding than lightly loaded ones. Horse-drawn wagons, and then motor lorries, have posed the main challenge to road structures. By dint of continuing research and experimentation, the problem of road wear has been largely solved; metalling is gradually being made denser and thicker, while axle weight limits keep in check the damaging effect of heavy vehicles. Even so, work continues to make the process of road-building more economical, and to cut down the delays to traffic caused by the need for maintenance and repair.

But there is another threat which may not be subject to a technical solution, namely the relentless rise of car ownership. While cars pose less of a problem than do lorries for road *strength*, they put a severe strain on road *capacity*, the ability of a network to allow traffic to move freely. Looked at from a historical perspective the growth in traffic is extraordinary and unprecedented. In the first few years of the twentieth century there were about 200,000 licensed vehicles, nearly all of them horse-drawn wagons, carriages and cabs. Though steam-powered vehicles were in evidence, there were only a few thousand, while the number of vehicles powered by internal combustion totalled just a hundred or so. Though the mix may have varied, the total number of vehicles had probably remained fairly stable for over a century. Yet, in a further 15 years, the number of petrol and diesel vehicles had passed the 200,000 mark, and while horse- and steam-powered vehicles slowly declined, the number of vehicles powered by internal combustion continued to grow spectacularly. It rose by no less than a factor of 10 in the next 20 years, reaching 2.5 million by 1935. Roads collapsed under the strain and congestion, always a problem at the centre of large towns, began to spread. In response, some new roads were built, and grand plans began to appear for large, new roads in towns. Yet what has happened since makes even these numbers seem insignificant. The number of vehicles had risen by a further factor of 10 by 1995, and has now passed the 30 million mark. Within a century, the private car has allowed almost everyone to share the personal travel freedom previously available only to a few.

But that freedom has come at a price: danger, noise, congestion, chemical pollution and the sheer impact and visual intrusion of vehicles affect everyone, whether they have a car or not. As a society we have sought to alleviate some of these effects, for example, on safety, by developing good design of the road environment, driver education and the introduction of laws on seat-belt wearing, speed and drink-driving. The annual toll of fatalities has fallen to less than half the peaks of around 8000 in 1940 and 1960. Though this improvement is only gradual in terms of overall numbers, it is dramatic in terms of fatalities *per vehicle*, which is now less than 3 per cent of what it was in 1920. But to continue this improvement in the face of yet more vehicles on the road will require continuing pressure on drivers to conform to the law and good practice, pressure which is often resented by motorists and their representatives. Similarly, the noise and chemical pollution caused per vehicle can be gradually reduced by good design and improved technology, but, as with road safety, increasing numbers make the total impact hard to control. There is also the problem of the conflicting interests of different road users, as walkers, cyclists, bus passengers and car drivers compete for attention and priority. But it may be the problem of congestion which is the most difficult to solve; there is simply not enough road space to go round.

One way to look at this is to imagine all vehicles spaced evenly along every piece of public road in the country. In 1909, there were less than two vehicles for every mile of road. Since then, the total length of road has risen by about 40 per cent, as new estate roads, bypasses and motorways have been added to the network. However, vehicle numbers have risen a hundredfold, so we now have over 120 vehicles per mile, or one every 14yds. Thus, if you were standing by one of these vehicles which were stationed evenly across the road network, in 1909 you would probably not have been able to see the next vehicle in the line, while today vehicles would fill every road, as far as the eye could see, in all directions (73, 74).

So why not build more roads? In purely technical terms, for inter-urban travel, it might be possible to provide sufficient road capacity, by a huge programme of widening existing roads and building new ones. Careful attention to gradients, curvature, lane width and junction design has allowed modern motorways to carry vastly more traffic than conventional roads, so it might be reasonable to say that, if we built enough of them, almost any amount of traffic could be carried. The limit is purely environmental; we would need to decide how prepared we were to put up with such a road-building programme. But when it comes to towns, there is a much more practical limit. This has been known since the publication of the Buchanan Report in 1963; the findings showed that, even with the most drastic and comprehensive redevelopment, not everyone who wishes to drive to or within a large town, would ever be able to do it without causing major congestion. This did not stop the report advocating going as far as possible towards this goal, and some spectacular, and controversial efforts have been made along these lines. For example, urban motorways have been built

73 Elborough Street, south-west London, taken in about 1900, showing numerous people and no vehicles. *Courtesy ICE*

since then, but public opposition has meant that no towns have attempted the major changes which the report suggested would be worthwhile. When it comes to the crunch, we do not seem to want our built environment to be completely taken over by our cars.

Some improved capacity has been achieved by design, such as the use of mini roundabouts, coordinated traffic signals etc. But the fact remains that traffic is growing faster than we can provide space for it; perhaps we may have to resort to tolling once more. When this was previously tried on a large scale, during the turnpike era, tolls were meant to raise money for road-building and repair. The need to pay was highly resented, because people then, as now, thought that roads ought to be free to users, in other words, paid for by someone else. During the nineteenth century local government, and, increasingly in the twentieth, central government, took over responsibility for road-building and maintenance, paying for the work out of general taxes. What tolls remain have been confined to large bridges; for the most part we have been willing to pay these limited tolls (Skye Bridge users notwithstanding). Recently, there has been a return of tolls on roads, with the opening of the North Birmingham scheme, achieved without major problems. But new schemes and proposals for tolling are not primarily to

CONCLUSIONS AND SPECULATIONS

raise money, but to limit demand. While public reaction is still to be fully tested, the London Congestion Charging Scheme has demonstrated that, for the first time, there is a potential mechanism available for ensuring that traffic volume and road capacity can be made roughly compatible.

But whatever measures are taken to control traffic, and whatever technological fixes are required to limit its deleterious effects, it seems inevitable that cars, lots of them, are here to stay for the foreseeable future; the genie of personal transport has been let out of the bottle, and will be virtually impossible to get back in. Nevertheless it is important to encourage other modes of travel, such as walking, cycling and public transport, and also to avoid our built environment being skewed too much, so that driving becomes a necessity for more and more journeys, rather than an option.

But simply carrying forward existing trends, as we have just done, has sometimes proved rather a poor way of forecasting the future of roads and traffic. Anyone observing the congested wagon traffic in a fourth-century Romano-British town could not have predicted that, within a century, wheeled traffic would virtually

74 Elborough Street, south-west London, taken in 2000, showing no people and numerous vehicles. *Courtesy ICE*

disappear, not to return in numbers for nearly a millennium. Again, at the turn of the twentieth century, an expert on new technology at the time, even if correctly foreseeing that internal combustion would be the power source of the future, might reasonably have predicted that horse- and steam-power would be replaced, but with the total number of vehicles remaining roughly the same. After all, a century had elapsed since Trevithick's invention of the self-propelled vehicle, yet the total number of vehicles on the roads had not varied significantly. Yet, within another century, their numbers increased more than a hundredfold. So, perhaps, somewhere, there is, even now, a new discovery or a new trend getting underway which will, within a few decades, dramatically alter the traffic on our roads yet again.

When it comes to living with our roads, clearly the current level of traffic causes great annoyance to residents living alongside busy thoroughfares. While we value the mobility that cars bring us, and the goods which are carried by lorries, we resent their presence in large numbers near our homes. This comes to the surface when proposals are made to 'improve' a particular stretch of road or street, to make it better able to carry the traffic which uses it. We have seen the example of different residents along the A40 London to Oxford road, who have resented a series of such expansions for at least 70 years. It is as if the arrival of a proposal for road development confirms the fact that the future will only offer more of the same. Yet, paradoxically, if a new bypass is constructed to carry traffic elsewhere, it is not many decades before new residents are living alongside that also, nervously awaiting the inevitable call for further road expansion.

Our road history can have its lighter side. We have the appealing but misguided image of the Romans, building their roads straight, because their wagons lacked steering and so were unable to go round corners. Again, there is the account of the blind road-builder, John Metcalf, travelling from London to Yorkshire more quickly on foot, than could his friend, riding in a private horse-drawn coach. There is also the romantic view of writers like Hilaire Belloc, who clearly felt a strong connection with earlier times, as they tried to trace the course of ancient highways, a feeling we can share today. But what of modern roads – can they bring us a sense of romance? Surely the maelstrom of traffic must have driven out such a concept. I do not think it has. After all, it was not so long ago that Edward Platt's interviewee recalled being brought up in west London, living next to the Western Avenue (A40). She knew it as 'The Oxford Road' and remembers her childhood dreams of setting off along it to visit what seemed to her a semi-magical place. The road itself became imbued with the romance of the place it went to, a quality which many roads can still have today. Sometimes, just being on a road can bring a sense of satisfaction, even exhilaration, whether it be a major highway, snaking though spectacular scenery, a quiet country lane or a bustling city street.

CONCLUSIONS AND SPECULATIONS

75 A memorable encounter during a walk through the woods

Nowadays we have a wide range of modes to choose from, but, if we revert to the oldest, walking, we not only benefit our health, but have the chance of some surprising encounters along the way (75).

BIBLIOGRAPHY

Albert, W., 1979, 'Popular Opposition to Turnpike Trusts in Eighteenth-Century England', *Journal of Transport History*, n.s. 5.1, 1-17

Aldhouse-Green, S. *et al.*, 1992, 'Prehistoric Human Footprints from the Severn Estuary at Uskmouth and Magor Pill', *Archaeologia Cambrensis*, 14, 14-55

Aldin, C., 1986, *The Romance of the Road*, Bracken Books, London (first published in 1928)

Anderson, J.R.L. and Godwin, F., 1975, *The Oldest Road: An Exploration of the Ridgeway*, Windwood House, London

ARAL (Asphalt Road Association Limited), 1963, *Hot Rolled Asphalt Bases*, The Association, London (now Quarry Products Association)

Armstrong, J., Aldridge J., Boyes G., Mustow G. and Storey R., 2003, *Companion to Road Haulage History*, British Museum, London

Babtie, 1998, *Industrial Berkshire*, Babtie Group, produced for Berkshire County Council, Reading

Bagshawe, R.W., 1994, *Roman Roads*, Shire Publishing, Princes Risborough (first published in 1979)

Baldwin, P. and Baldwin, R. (eds), 2004, *The Motorway Achievement Volume 1, The British Motorway System: Visualisation, Policy and Administration*, Thomas Telford Press for the Motorway Archive Trust, London

Barber, R., 1999, *The Pastons, Family in the Wars of the Roses*, Bodell Press, Woodbridge (first published in 1986)

Barker, T.C., 1993, 'Slow Progress: Forty Years of Motoring Research', *Journal of Transport History*, 3rd series 14.2, 142-65

Beale, P., 2005, *England's Mail: Two Millennia of Letter Writing*, Tempus Publishing, Stroud

Bell, M. *et al.*, 2000, 'Prehistoric Intertidal Archaeology in the Welsh Severn Estuary', *CBA Research Report 120*, Council for British Archaeology, York

Belloc, H., 1924, *The Road*, Fisher Unwin, London

Bennett, P., 1983, 'The South-West Side of the St. George's Street Bath Building', in S.S. Frere and S. Stow, 1983, 324-33

Bird, A., 1969, *Roads and Vehicles*, Longman, Green, London

Bland, D.S., 1957, 'The Maintenance of Roads in Medieval England', *Planning Outlook*, 4.2, 5-15

Bressey, C. and Lutyens, E., 1938, *Highway Development Survey 1937 (Greater London)*, HMSO, London

Bridle, R. and Porter, J. (eds), 2002, *The Motorway Achievement Volume 2: Frontiers of Knowledge and Practice*, Thomas Telford Press for the Motorway Archive Trust, London

Bromwich, R., 1961, *Trioedd ynys Prydein (The Welsh Triads)*, University of Wales Press, Cardiff

Buchanan, C.D. *et al.*, 1963, *Traffic in Towns: A Study of the Long-Term Problems of Traffic in Urban Areas*, HMSO, London

Cameron, K., 1996, *English place-names*, Batsford, London

Chandler, J., 1993, *John Leland's Itinerary: Travels in Tudor England*, Alan Sutton, Stroud

Clark, G., 1965, 'Traffic in Stone Axe and Adze Blades', *Economic History Review*, n.s. 18.1, 1-28

Coles, B. and Coles, J., 1986, *Sweet Track to Glastonbury: The Somerset Levels in Prehistory*, Thames and Hudson, London

Colwill, D., 2004, 'Safety Research at the Transport Research Laboratory', in P. Baldwin and R. Baldwin (eds), *The Motorway Achievement Volume 1: The British Motorway System, Visualization, Policy and Administration*, Thomas Telford Press for the Motorway Archive Trust, London, 671-706

Cooke, S., 1930 (approx.), *This Motoring: Being the Romantic Story of the Automobile Association*, The Automobile Association, London

Crane, J.L.B., 1991, *We Made Trailers*, Anthony Nelson, Oswestry

Cron, F.W., 1974, 'Highway Design for Motor Vehicles – A Historical Review: Part 7, The Evolution of Highway Grade Design', *Public Roads*, 40.2, 78-86

Cunliffe, B., 1991, *Danebury, an Iron Age hillfort in Hampshire, Volume 4: the excavations 1979-88, the site*, *CBA Research Report 73*

–, 1995, *Danebury, an Iron Age hillfort in Hampshire, Volume 6: a hillfort community in perspective*, *CBA Research Report 102*

Davies, H.E.H., 2002, *Roads in Roman Britain*, Tempus, Stroud

BIBLIOGRAPHY

Edmonds, M., 1995, *Stone Tools and Society*, Batsford, London

Edwards, G.W., 1984, *Minor Rural Roads*, St David's University College, Lampeter

Fowler, P., 1998, 'Moving Through the Landscape', in P. Everson and T. Williamson (eds), *The Archaeology of Landscape*, Manchester University Press, Manchester, 25-41

Freeman, M.J., 1975, 'The Stage-coach System of South Hampshire, 1775-1851', *Journal of Historical Geography*, 163, 259-81

—, 1977, 'The Carrier System of South Hampshire, 1775-1851', *The Journal of Transport History*, n.s. 4.2, 61-85

Frere, S.S. and Stow, S. (eds), 1983, *The Archaeology of Canterbury: Excavations in the St. George's Street and Burgate Street Areas*, Kent Archaeological Society, Maidstone, for the Canterbury Archaeological Trust

Fulford, M.G., Rippon, S., Ford, S., Timby, J. and Williams, B., 1997, 'Silchester Excavations at the North Gate, on the North Wall and in the Northern Suburbs', *Britannia* 28, 87-168

Fulford, M.G. and Timby, J., 2000, *Late Iron Age and Roman Silchester: excavation on the site of the Forum/Basilica, 1977, 1980-86*, Britannia Monograph Series No. 15, London

Gallagher, W.E., 2004, 'Geometric design issues and the development of computing practice so as to affect policy', in P. Baldwin and R. Baldwin (eds), *The Motorway Achievement Volume 1: The British Motorway System, Visualization, Policy and Administration*, Thomas Telford Press for the Motorway Archive Trust, London, 387-436

Gantz, J., 1976, *The Mabinogion: Translated and Introduced by Jeffrey Gantz*, Penguin, London

Gerhold, A., 1993, 'Packhorses and Wheeled Vehicles in England, 1550-1800', *Journal of Transport History*, 14.1, 1-26

Gibson, T., 2001, *Road Haulage by Motor in Britain: The First Forty Years*, Ashgate, Aldershot

Grimes, W.F., 1951, 'The Jurassic Way', in Grimes, W.F. (ed.), *Aspects of Archaeology in Britain and Beyond*, Edwards, London, 144-71

Guest, E., 1857, 'The Four Roman Ways', *The Archaeological Journal.* 14, 99-118

Guttmann, E.B.A. and Last, J., 2000, 'Late Bronze Age Landscape at South Hornchurch, Essex', *Proceedings of the Prehistoric Society*, 66, 319-60

Harrison, D., 2004, *The Bridges of Medieval England: Transport and Society 400-1800*, Clarendon Press, Oxford

Harrison, S., 2004, 'The Icknield Way: Some Questions', *The Archaeological Journal*, 160, 1-22

Hart, H.W., 1962, 'The Sedan Chair as a means of Public Conveyance', *Journal of Transport History*, 5.4, 205-218

Haslam, J., 1984, (ed.), *Anglo-Saxon Towns in Southern England*, Phillimore, Chichester

Herbert, Col. H.E., 1971, *Trial Without Jury. A Road Problem: Facts, Farce and the Future*, Carfax, Oxford

Higman, D., 2002, *A Brief History of the Bicycle*, Internet publication

Hiller, J., Petts, D. and Allen, T., 2002, 'Discussion of the Anglo-Saxon Archaeology,' in S. Foreman, J. Hiller and D. Petts (eds), *Gathering the People, Settling the Land: Thames Valley Landscape Monograph No. 14*, Oxford Archaeology, Oxford, 57-72

Hindle, P., 2001, *Roads and Tracks for Historians*, Phillimore, Chichester (first edition, published in 1993, with the title *Roads, Tracks and their Interpretation*)

Hogg, G., 1967, *Blind Jack of Knaresborough: Road-builder extraordinary*, Phoenix House, London

Hooke, D., 1981, *Anglo-Saxon Landscapes of the West Midlands: the Charter Evidence*, B.A.R. British Series 95, Oxford

Inglis, H.R.G., 1899-1907, *The Contour Road Map of England: Western Division (including Wales; South-East Division; Northern Division*, Gall and Inglis, Edinburgh

–, 1903, *The Contour Road Map of Scotland*, Gall and Inglis, Edinburgh

Jusserand, J.J., 1889, *English Wayfaring Life in the Middle Ages*, Ernest Benn (this edition by Cedric Chivers, Bath, 1970)

Kain, R.J., Chapman, J. and Oliver, R.R., 2004, *The Enclosure Maps of England and Wales, 1595-1918*, Cambridge University Press, Cambridge

Kennerell, E.J.R., 1958, 'Roads from the Beginning', *Journal of the Institution of Highway Engineers*, 5(3), 177-205

Law, H., 1855, *The Rudiments of Constructing and Repairing Common Roads*, John Weale, London (Reprinted in 1970 by Kingsmead, Bath)

Lay, M.G., 1992, *Ways of the World: A History of the World's Roads and the Vehicles that Used Them*, Rutgers University Press, New Jersey

McAdam, J.L., 1819, Evidence to the Parliamentary Select Committee on Highways of the Kingdom, 23 (Given on 4 March 1819)

–, 1825, *Observations on the Management of Trusts and the Care of Turnpike Roads etc.*, London

McGowan, C., 2004, *The Rainhill Trials: The Greatest Contest of Industrial Britain and the Birth of Commercial Rail*, Little Brown, London

Margary, I.D., 1973, *Roman Roads in Britain*, third edition, John Baker, London (first published in two volumes, 1956/7)

Marples, M., 1960, *Shanks's Pony: A Study of Walking*, Country Book Club, London

Martin, G.H., 1975, 'Road Travel in the Middle Ages: Some Journeys by the Warden and Fellows of Merton College, Oxford, 1350-1470', *Journal of Transport History*, n.s. 3, 159-78

Michell, J., 2004, 'Traditions of Ancient Surveying in Britain', in R. Heath and J. Michell (eds), *The Measure of Albion*, Bluestone, St. Dogmaels, Pembrokeshire

Millar, T.G., 1977, *Long Distance Paths of England and Wales*, David and Charles, Newton Abbot

Morley, F., 1961, *The Great North Road*, Hutchinson, London

O'Connor, C., 1993, *Roman Bridges*, Cambridge University Press, Cambridge

Ogilby, J., 1675, *Britannia: Or an Illustration of the Kingdom of England and Dominion of Wales by a Graphical and Historical Description of the Principal Roads Thereof*, printed by the author (facsimile reprint by Duckham, London, 1939)

Parsons, E.J.S., and Stenton, Sir F., 1958, *The Map of Great Britain, circa 1360, known as the Gough Map: An Introduction to the Facsimile*, Oxford University Press for the Bodleian Library and the Royal Geographical Society, Oxford

Pawson, E., 1977, *Transport and Economy: The Turnpike Roads of Eighteenth Century Britain*, Academy Press, London

Peddie, J., 1997, *Conquest: The Roman Invasion of Britain*, Sutton, Stroud (first published 1987)

Philip, B. and Garrod, D., 1994, 'Prehistoric Wooden Trackway at Greenwich', *Kent Archaeological Review*, 117 (1994)

Pierce, P., 2001, *Old London Bridge: The Story of the Oldest Inhabited Bridge in Europe*, Headline Books, London

Piggott, S., 1992, *Wagon, Chariot and Carriage: Symbol and Status in the History of Transport*, Thames and Hudson, New York

Platt, E., 2001, *Leadville*, Picador, London (first published 2000)

Pollard, J., 2003, *Seven Ages of Britain: A History of the British People from the Ice Age to the Industrial Revolution*, Hodder and Stoughton, London

Pryor, F., 1991, *English Heritage Book of Flag Fen Prehistoric Fenland Centre*, Batsford/ English Heritage, London

Quartermaine, J., Trinder, B. and Turner, R., 2003, *Thomas Telford's Holyhead Road: the A5 in North Wales*, Council for British Archaeology CBA Monograph 135, York

Reader, W.J., 1980, *MACADAM: The McAdam Family and Turnpike Roads, 1798-1861*, Heineman, London

RRL, 1962, *Bituminous Materials in Road Construction*, HMSO, London, for Road Research Laboratory, Crowthorne

–, 1965, *Road Note 29: A Guide to the Structural Design of Flexible and Rigid Pavements for New Roads*, HMSO, London, for Road Research Laboratory, Crowthorne

Rolt, L.T.C., 1985, *Thomas Telford: The acclaimed biography of the Father of Civil Engineering*, Penguin Books, London (first published in 1958)

Salter, R.J., 1994, *Highway Design and Construction*, second edition, Macmillan, Basingstoke (first published 1979)

Salisbury, G.T., 1948, *Street Life in Medieval England*, Pen-in-Hand, Oxford (first published 1939)

Scales, R.J., 2002, 'Footprint Tracks at Goldcliff East 2002', in *Annual Report of the Severn Estuary Levels Research Committee, Volume 13: Archaeology in the Severn Estuary 2002*, SELRC, Bristol, 31-35

Smith, A.D.W., 2004, 'A History of the "Motorway Concept" before such construction began in the UK', in P. Baldwin and R. Baldwin (eds), *The Motorway Achievement Volume 1, The British Motorway System: Visualisation, Policy and Administration*, Thomas Telford Publications, London

Sprey, J., 2004, *The History of the Pedestrians Association: A Seventy-Five Year Campaign for Living Streets*, Living Streets, London

Starkie, D., 1982, *The Motorway Age: Road and Traffic Policies in Post-War Britain*, Pergamon, Oxford

Sullivan, D., 1999, *Ley Lines: A Comprehensive Guide to Alignments*, Judy Piatkus, London

Taylor, C., 1979, *Roads and Tracks of Britain*, Dent, London

Taylor, W., 1996, *The Military Roads of Scotland*, House of Lochar, Colonsay (revised edition: first published 1976)

Taylor, S. (ed.), 2002, *The Moving Metropolis: A History of London's Transport since 1800*, Laurence\King Publishing, London (first published 2001)

Thomas, C. and Rackham, J., 1996, 'Brancote Green, Bermondsey; a Bronze Age Trackway and palaeo-environmental sequence', *Proceedings of the Prehistoric Society*, 62, 221-53

Timmins, G., 2003, 'Techniques of Easing Road Gradients during the Industrial Revolution: A Case Study of Textile Lancashire', *Industrial Archaeology Review*, 25.2, 97-117

Timperley, H.W. and Brill, E., 2005, *Ancient Trackways of Wessex*, Nonsuch, Stroud (first published 1965)

Tomalin, C., 2002, *Samuel Pepys: The Unequalled Self*, Viking, London Transport Statistics, see www.dft.org.uk. Also see *Statistical Abstracts of Great Britain* (later called *Annual Abstract of Statistics*), HMSO, for nineteenth- and early twentieth-century data

Watkins, A., 1925, *The Old Straight Track*, latest reprint by Abacus in 1994, London

Webb, S. and Webb, B., 1920, *English Local Government: The Story of the King's Highway*, Longman Green, London

Williamson, T. and Bellamy L., 1983, *Ley Lines in Question*, World's Work, Tadworth

Wright, C.J., 1971, *A guide to the Pilgrim's Way and the North Downs Way*, Constable, London

Wynn, J., 2003, *Wynns, The First 100 Years*, Forward House Publishing, Stafford

Yates, D.T., forthcoming, *Land, Power and Prestige: Bronze Age field systems in Southern England*, English Heritage

APPENDIX

TABLE 3 Chronological list of significant events in the history of roads

DATE	ITEM	DESCRIPTION AND COMMENT
9,000–4,000 BC	**Mesolithic period** (Middle Stone Age)	Hunter-gatherers in Britain. Footprints found on foreshore of River Severn. Tracks probably based on routes used by quarry animals.
4,000–2,000 BC	**Neolithic period** (New Stone Age)	First farming. Tracks established for reaching fields and pastures from settlements. Stone and timber monuments. Timber trackways. Suggested origin of long-distance tracks.
2,000–800 BC	**Bronze Age**	Need for tracks to access sources of metal ore and metal-working sites. Timber trackways.

800 BC – AD 43	**Iron Age** (in England and Wales. Extended to eighth century in Western Isles of Scotland)	Hillforts and *oppida*. First appearance of metalled streets, for example at Danebury and Silchester.
Fourth century BC	Twelve Tables: Early codification of Roman law	A *via* must be wide enough for a vehicle to pass along; normal width should be 8 *pedes*, but increased to 12 *pedes* on bends.
AD 43–420	**Roman period**: Britain becomes part of Roman Empire as province of *Britannia*	Network of over 6,000 miles (10,000km) of surveyed roads, with widespread use of the raised *agger*, metalling and drainage.
43–100	Roman roads	Roman road system takes shape in Britain, first as military network, then mainly transfers to civilian use except in west and north.
429–35	Theodosian Code 5.47 Codification of Roman Law by Emperor Theodosius	Weight limit of 1000lb (450kg) for wagons. The objective may have been to limit wear on roads, but extent of enforcement is not clear. For sources on the Code, see Oxford Classical Dictionary, 3rd edition, p.1501.
529	Code of Justinian. Further codification of Roman law	Definitions of a *via* as a public right of way, with minimum width requirements for vehicles; 8 *pedes* for one-way traffic.
420–1066	**Early medieval period**: Anglo-Saxon and Danish rulers within England, local kings in Wales and Scotland	Roman roads still in use, though maintenance often neglected. Anglo-Saxon names for Roman roads, e.g. Watling Street. Other roads with names such as Saltway and Portway, for access to salt producing areas and markets respectively.

APPENDIX

1000 approx.	London Bridge	First timber bridge across the Thames to replace the one which was in place during the Roman period.
1042–66	Laws of Edward the Confessor	Codification of laws, possibly originated earlier by Edward's brother, Edmund. The King's Peace applied to four important roads, which thus became known as the Four Royal Roads: these were Watling Street, Foss Way, Icknield Street and Ermine Street. This provision meant that any crime committed on them would be tried by the King's own officers and not by a local court.
1066–1485	**Medieval period** (Middle Ages): Normans, Houses of Plantagenet and York	Growth of town streets and inter-urban links. Basis of modern road network takes shape. Widespread bridge-building. Though less attention paid to roads, limited use of wheeled vehicles avoided major problems.
1100–35	Laws of Henry I	1) A royal highway is one which cannot be closed off, leading to a city fortress, castle or royal town. 2) Assaults against travellers on the King's highway come under his jurisdiction. 3) A town has as many main streets as main gates, used for collecting tolls. 4) Width of highway should be sufficient for two carts to pass, two herdsmen to touch goads across it, or 16 armed knights to ride abreast. Item 2 effectively extends the King's Peace to all major roads (see 1042 above).
1176	London Bridge	Start of building first masonry bridge across the Thames, known as Old London Bridge.

1199	Berwick Bridge	Building of bridge over River Tweed. Numerous collapses, including one in 1294 which led to a 50-year gap before harbour dues were used to finance the building of another. But fresh collapses followed.
c.1250	Matthew Paris, medieval cartographer	Most of his maps are itineraries, not showing course of roads. However, one map does show the Four Royal Roads, albeit in diagrammatic form (see 1042 above), even though by this time they had lost their unique legal status (see 1100 above).
1282	London Bridge tax	Following long period of misappropriation of tolls, London Bridge was impassable. Edward I was forced to raise a national tax to pay for renovations.
1284	Statute of Westminster	13 Ed I, St 2, C 5. First Statute of Westminster. Main roads to have trees and bushes cleared for a width of 200ft (61m) from each side to deter robbers. Lord of Manor liable for damages if he failed to carry out such work and a robbery occurred on the highway.
c.1350	Gough Map	Shows roads linking towns, forming a pattern of roads which is similar to the modern pre-motorway network.
1353	London street paving	27 Ed III. Patent, deploring state of the London street from Temple Bar to Westminster, and ordering it to be paved. Three years later City authorities levied a tax on goods entering London, to raise money for road repairs.

APPENDIX

1416	Abingdon Bridge	Building of the bridge attracted the Gloucester Road away from Wallingford and was recorded in a famous poem. By this time the Thames already had bridges up and downstream of Abingdon, though London Bridge was still the only river crossing in the capital.
1485-1688	**Post-medieval period** (or early modern) Tudors, Stuarts	Stability and economic growth, after fourteenth-century plague years and civil war. Beginning of a rising fashion for travelling in wheeled vehicles, possibly encouraged by Queen Elizabeth I who was the first monarch to use a coach for the state opening of Parliament. Pressure on roads grew rapidly towards the end of the period.
1530	Bridges and approach roads	22 Henry VIII c. 5. Justices of the Peace to raise taxes for bridge-building and repair. Applies also to approach roads within 300ft (91m).
1556	Parish responsibility for roads	2/3 Philip and Mary c. 8. Establishment of parish-based system for road maintenance, to replace an ill-defined responsibility on landowners. Surveyors to be elected to work with Church Wardens. Four days a year to be specified for all parishioners to provide labour and materials for road repairs. This measure was no more successful than its predecessor and, after several later Acts to modify it, was replaced by a turnpike system, financed by tolls.

1562	Parish responsibility for roads	5 Eliz c. 13. Continuation of 1556 Act for further 20 years. Increased powers for surveyors to remove rubbish from roads, acquire stone from quarries for repairs, stop up or divert streams, scour ditches and keep down height of hedges. Days required for road works to be increased to 6 per year.
1575	Landowners to contribute more to road repairs	18 Eliz 10. Doubts about Acts of 1556 and 1562. More contribution required from landowners alongside roads.
1596	Levy on transport of coal and iron in Weald	39 Eliz c. 19. Levy on every load of coal or iron from mine and mills of Sussex, Suffolk and Kent, together with provision of road-making materials.
1621	James I	Proclamation limiting weight of wagons to 1 ton. First Turnpike Bill, for toll-gate on Great North Road, was defeated on grounds that it was an unacceptable new tax.
1635	Postal Service	The Royal Postal Service made available to the public.
1662	London Streets	13/14 Ch II c. 2. Streets of London and Westminster: appointment of Commissioners, control of encroachment, street paving, lighting and cleaning, licensing Hackney cabs (limited numbers, fares etc.), widening of certain streets with compensation for houses demolished, etc.

APPENDIX

1662	Use of limits on number of horses	13/14 Ch II c. 6. Wagon wheels not to be less than 4in (10cm) wide, weight limit 1 ton 10cwt (1.5t) in summer, 1 ton in winter (because there were no weigh-bridges, weight limit was enforced by limiting number of horses to seven).
1663	Turnpike Acts	15 Ch II, c. 1. First Turnpike Act. Preamble describes burden on parishes from heavy traffic on road from East Anglia to London. Toll gates to be set up on Great North Road at Wadesmill, Caxton and Stilton. Powers needed to be confirmed by new acts every 20 years or so.
1671	Alignment of horses	22 Ch II c. 12. Amendment of 1662 act to restrict number of horses in line to five; any more must be harnessed in pairs. Obligation of landowners along paved streets in Southwark for maintenance.
1696	Turnpike Acts	7/8 Will III, c. 4, c. 26. Second and third Turnpike Acts, Shenfield–Harwich and Wymondham–Attleborough. From now on there are usually several each year until 1800.
1696	Alignment of horses	7/8 Will III, c. 29. Problems of 1671 act not limiting total number of horses and that horses in pairs were sometimes harnessed so that they walked in line with wheels, increasing rutting. Limit of eight horses altogether, harnessed in pairs within line of wagon wheels.
1708	Extra horses on hills	6 Anne c. 29. Number of horses limited to six except on hills.

1710	Driving on the left	Mayor of London orders that traffic on London Bridge should keep to the left, to make efficient use of newly widened carriageway. See 1835.
1711	Abuse of provision for extra horses on hills	9 Anne c. 18. Repeal of provision in 1708 Act for extra horses to be used on hills, because of abuse with these horses being used also on the flat.
1715	Number of horses	1 Geo I, St. 2, c. 11. Permitted number of horses reduced to five.
1718	Numbers of horses	5 Geo I, c. 20. Heavy carts and wagons still causing problem. Limit of three horses pulling vehicle with iron-bound wheels. Exemptions for large indivisible loads (marble, timber etc.) and closed carriages for the nobility.
1719	Overloading	6 Geo I, c. 6. In absence of weigh-bridges, overloading controlled by limiting number of sacks on each wagon.
1728	Wade's Roads	General Wade appointed Commander-in-Chief in Scotland, beginning his association with the building of a network of military roads. Recalled in 1740 but roads programme continued under Major Caulfeild.
1741	Weighing vehicles	14 Geo II, c. 42. Weight limit raised to 3 tons. Authority to use weigh-bridges to enforce the limit.
1753	Turnpikes	The year with maximum number of Turnpike Acts, at 37.

APPENDIX

1761	London Bridge	All houses on the bridge are removed to make more room for traffic.
1766	Features on roads	7 Geo III c. 40. Consolidation of previous measures, including weight limits, wheel width, provision of weigh-bridges, setting up of signposts and milestones etc.
1773	Limits on number of horses pulling wagons	13 Geo III, c. 78. Eight horses allowed for wagons with 9in (225cm) wheels, fewer for narrower wheels. Width of roads to market towns to be 24ft (7.3m).
1773	Weight limits on turnpikes	13 Geo III, c. 84. Weight limit on turnpike roads to be 8 tons, wheels must be 16in (41cm) wide.
1799	Highland Roads	Review of military roads, showed that 599 miles (964km) and nearly 1000 bridges had been built.
1800	Trevithick's wheel grip experiment	Richard Trevithick detached a wagon from its horse, then pressed down on the spokes of one wheel to see if there was sufficient grip to propel the vehicle forward.
1801	Highland Roads in Scotland	Thomas Telford appointed to survey Scottish Highland Roads. Though the army had completed a network of military roads, Telford found them too steep and rough for civilian use.
1801	Trevithick's first steam vehicle	Trevithick demonstrates the first successful steam-powered vehicle, 'The Cambourne Flyer'.

1806	Shape of wagon wheels	Parliamentary Committee to examine effect of wheel shape on wear. Experiments with conical and elliptical profiles.
1808	State of the Highways	Parliamentary Report. Opposes central control of roads, even though it is known that some Turnpike Trusts waste money on inefficient repairs. Further discussion of the shape of wagon wheels.
1816	McAdam	John McAdam appointed surveyor of roads round Bristol.
1819	Scottish Highland Roads	In 18 years Thomas Telford built or realigned 1140 miles (1835km) roads and completed over 1000 bridges.
1819	Parliamentary Committee on Roads	John McAdam gives evidence; states he would rather build a road over a bog than over rock.
1822	Summer and winter weight limits and wheel widths	3 Geo IV, c. 126. Maximum weight 6 tons 10cwt (6.5t) in summer, 6 tons (6t) in winter, with 9in (22.5cm) wheels. Lower maximum for narrower wheels. Limit on projection of nails from wheel rim. Locked wheels on hill descents must be fitted with skid pans or slippers.
1834	Wheel width and springs	4/5 Will IV, c. 81. Relaxation of weight restrictions for wagons with wide wheels and fitted with springs.

1835	Driving on the left	5/6 Will IV, c. 50. Traffic to keep to left, though no powers given for enforcement. Groups of parishes or districts can take over running of their roads.
1836	Turnpikes Acts	Last of 942 Turnpike Acts in England and Wales, with a total length of approximately 22,000 miles (35,400km).
1845	Pneumatic tyres	Invention of pneumatic tyres, though initially only suitable for bicycles; not used on vehicles until twentieth century.
c.1850	Decline of road travel	Long-distance road travel, both for passengers and freight, declines in face of competition from railways.
1851	Holyhead Road	Parliamentary Commissioners end financial support, following completion of rail link to Holyhead.
1861	Tolls for steam-powered vehicles	Locomotive Act, c. 70. Tolls for locomotives at the rate of 1 horse equivalent for each 2 tons (2t) of loco weight, plus 1 horse equivalent for each wheel of trailers. Upper weight limit 12 tons (12t), with complex relationship between weight limits and wheel shape and diameter. One sixth added to weight limit if vehicle fitted with springs.
1865	Red Flag Act	Locomotive on Roads Act, c. 83. Three attendants required for a steam road locomotive, plus one for each trailer. One attendant to walk on front with red flag to give warning. Speed limit 4mph (2mph in towns). Width limit 9ft (2.7m).

1872	Local Government Board	Public Health Act authorises the Local Government Board to begin taking over responsibility for roads run by Turnpike Trusts.
1878	Highway districts. Damage to bridges etc.	Highways and Locomotive Act, c. 77. Highway Districts to take over turnpike roads. Weight limit 14 tons (14t) unless authorised, but such authority liable for bridge repair costs if damaged by such loads.
1878	Cyclists	Bicyclists Touring Club was founded to counter hostile attitude of horse-riders and wagon drivers. Later became the Cyclists' Touring Club.
1896	Relaxation of Red Flag Act	Locomotives on Roads Act, c. 36. Provision for Light Locomotives, weighing less than 3 tons (3t) unladen, or 4 tons (4t) with trailer. Speed limit up to 14mph if authorised locally. First use of speed limit linked to weight of vehicle. Red Flag provision for heavy locos not repealed until 1930.
1903	Light mechanised vehicles recognised in law. Licensing of drivers and vehicles, speed limits etc.	Motor Car Act, c. 36. Update of categories to take account of new light vehicles with steam and IC engines. Licensing of drivers and registration of vehicles. Speed limit of 20mph, though local authorities could impose lower limits in their areas.

APPENDIX

1904	Heavy Motor Car Order Cmnd 1809	Issued to local authorities by Local Government Board. Heavy Motor Car (i.e. a lorry or bus) defined as being between 2 and 5 tons unladen (6.5 with trailer). First use of axle weight limits, set at 8 tons, with overall limit at 12 tons. Registration of drivers. Speed limit 8mph, with 12 allowed if using pneumatic tyres and an axle weight of less than 6 tons.
1905	AA	Formation of the Automobile Association.
1915	Licensed vehicles	Number of licences for motor vehicles overtakes that for horse-drawn ones for the first time (200,000 each).
1919	Ministry of Transport (MoT) created	Ministry of Transport Act, c. 50. New ministry takes over national policy on roads, vehicles and traffic (replacing the Roads Board), though local authorities remained responsible for roads in their areas.
1923	Vehicle licences	Number of licensed motor vehicles passes 1m.
1927	Road markings	First use of single white line to delineate carriageway.
1928	Royal Commission on Transport, Cmnd. 365	Speed limits widely ignored; recommends complete abolition, with law on dangerous driving to control behaviour.
1929	PA	Formation of the Pedestrians Association, now renamed 'Living Streets'.

1930	Speed limits Vehicle categories etc.	Road Traffic Act, c. 43. Abolition of speed limits for cars, 30mph or less for other vehicles, depending on weight. Definitions of vehicles based on unladen weight: Light Motor Cars (below 3 tons), Heavy Motor Cars, (3-7.5 tons). These two categories are still in use in legislation, to define cars or light vans, and lorries or buses respectively. Definition of a vehicle carrying part of the load (articulated vehicle). Powers to issue Vehicle Construction and Use Regulations and for authorisation of Special Vehicle Types. Drivers' hours limits etc.
1931	Motor Vehicle Construction and Use and Special Types Regulations.	First use of C&U provisions, for specifying vehicle lighting, brakes, tyres, suspension etc. and Special Types for heavy, wide or long vehicles. Format still in use. Trailers could carry 40 tons, higher only with special permission. Relaxation of rules on attendants for articulated vehicles, thus giving them a commercial advantage over rigid lorries pulling trailers.
1933	TRL	Formation of the Road Research Laboratory (RRL), now known as the Transport Research Laboratory (TRL).
1934	Pedestrian crossings	Road Traffic Act. First dedicated pedestrian crossings introduced, marked by flashing spherical lamps, known as Belisha beacons after the then Minister of Transport, Lord Hore-Belisha.
1934	Speed limit	Local authorities given power to introduce 30mph speed limit in 'built-up areas', defined by level of street lighting.

APPENDIX

1935	Ribbon Development	The Act provides powers to limit ribbon development along main roads.
1936	Trunk Roads	Trunk Road Act transferred direct responsibility for main roads from local authorities to MoT. First direct government control of any roads since the nineteenth century (Holyhead Road).
1938	Greater London Development Survey	Sir Charles Bressey (Engineer) and Sir Edwin Lutyens (Architect). Problem of traffic access to arterial roads and ribbon development along them. Need to build new roads, perhaps alongside railways. Need for bridges and roundabouts accepted. Roads need to be wide enough for footways, cycleways and service roads alongside; 140ft (43m) recommended.
1939	First road surface trial	A 1-mile (1.6km) section of the Colnbrook Bypass (A4) in Buckinghamshire was used to test 700 specifications of bituminous road surface.
1940	Road deaths	Annual fatalities peak at over 8000, though this figure is nearly reached again in 1960s.
1945	Bridge collapse	Collapse of River Ure Bridge on A5 at Boroughbridge as heavy trailer passed over it.
1951	Pedestrian crossings	Zebra crossings introduced.
1954	Vehicle licences	Number of licensed motor vehicles passes 5 million.

1958	First Motorway	Britain's first motorway, the Preston Bypass, was opened. This now forms part of M6.
1959	M1	First section of M1 opened by Ernest Marples, Minister of Transport.
1960	MoT Test	First introduction of MoT test for vehicles over 10 years old.
1965	Severn Bridge	The first Severn Bridge was opened to carry the M4 into Wales.
1965	Speed limits	First use of national speed limits on derestricted roads since 1930.
1973	London Bridge	Present London Bridge is opened. John Rennie's bridge, opened in 1831, is dismantled and re-erected at Lake Havasu City, Arizona, USA.
1977	Cycling	Setting up of SUSTRANS and opening of the first section of the National Cycle Network, now extending to over 10,000 miles (16,000km).
1991	Speed limits	20mph zones introduced.
2000	Cycle Network	The National Cycle Network is opened.
2002	Vehicle licences	Number of licensed motor vehicles passes 30 million.
2002	Lorry weights	Maximum weight for vehicle with 6 axles (articulated or pulling a trailer) raised to 44t.

INDEX

Figures in bold denote illustrations.

Abingdon, Berks.,
    building of medieval bridge at, 99
    need for bridge at, 145
    views of present bridge, **49**, **50**
    visit by John Leland to, 99
Abington, Lanarkshire,
    historic and recent views of, **23**, **24**
    motorway near, **36**
Act of Union with Ireland, 61
agger (role of in Roman roads), 77
Albert, W., 54, 146
Aldhouse-Green, S., 20
Aldin, C., 130
Allan, T., 79
Anderson, J., 31
Anglesey, 61
Anglo-Saxon period,
    course of roads in, 45
    lack of evidence for tracks, 79
    road names, 47
Antonine Wall, 42
ARAL, **38**
Archaeology South-East, 11
Armstrong, J., 143
asphalt (use in road-making), 88
    make-up, 94
    manufactured, 89
    minor roads, 95

    natural deposits, 88
    natural, 157
    use over concrete, 95
attitudes to traffic, 149, 162
Austen, J., 128
Autobahn, Germany (view of in 1937), **60**
Avebury, Wilts, 31, 32, 50
Axle weight,
    impact on road wear, 94, 144
    limits on, **71**

Babtie, 87
Bagshawe, R., 40
Balaculish, Highland Region,
    ferry at, 61
    views of bridge at, **29**, **30**
Baldwin, P., 73
Baldwin, R., 73
Barber Greene carpeting machine, **44**
Barber, R., 133
Barker, T., 133, 137
Bath Road (watering of), 87
Beale, P., 133
Bell, M., 11, 21
Bellamy, L., 37
Belloc, H., 21, 29, **9**
Bennett, P., 80, **41**
Berwyn, Denbighshire, bridges at, **51**

Bewley, J., 11
Biggar Museum, Lanarkshire, 11, **23**
Biggleswade, Beds., 53
Bird, A., 135, 137
Birdlip Hill, Glos. (gradient at), 110
Birmingham (motorway links to), 70
Bitumen (use on road-making), 88
Bland, D., 145
blocks (use in road-making), 90
Bodleian Library, Oxford, 48
Boswell, J. (overturn of carriage), 146
Bressey, C., 71, 139
bridges,
    Abingdon, Berks., 99, 145, 157, **49**, **50**
    at Berwyn, Denbighshire, **51**
    Balaculish, Highland Region, **29**, **30**
    Berwick upon Tweed, Nthumb., 100
    Boroughbridge, Yorks. (collapse under heavy load), 102
    effect of poor maintenance, 100
    history of, 98
    London to Gloucester road, 99
    London, 102
    medieval, 157
    Menai, Anglesey, 66, **32**
    over river Dee, **52**
    Stamford, Lincs., **18**
Bridle, R., 12, 73, 98, 110, 113, 114, 116, 119, **57**, **61**
Brill, E., 29
Bristol (motorway links to), 71
British Library 11, **11**
Bromwich, R., 35
Brown, H., 11
Buchanan, Sir C., 72, 159, **37**
Bury St Edmonds, Suffolk, 33

Caerleon, Newport, 36, 41
Caernarfon, Gwynedd, 36
Caistor, Norfolk, 42
Caithness, 33
Cambridge (motorway links to), 71
Cameron, K., 46
Canterbury, Kent
    Becket's shrine, 29
    St George's Street Roman bathhouse, 80, **41**
Canterbury Archaeological Trust, 11
Carlisle, Cumbria, 50
Carmarthen, Carms., 36
Caulfeild, Major W., 61
cement and concrete,
    use in road-making, 89
    expansion joints, 90
    experiments in the Strand, London, 90
    Roman road in Lincoln, 89
Chandler, J., 99
Chapman, J., 58
Charvil, Berkshire, 87
Cheltenham, Glos. (experiments with tarmacadam), 88
Chester, Cheshire, 33
Chippenham, Wilts., 50
Chrimes, M., 12
Cirencester, Glos., 41
Clark, G., 32

cobbles (use in road-making), 90
Colchester, Essex, 42, 78
Coles, B., 21
Coles, J., 21
Colwill, D., 117
concrete (see 'cement and concrete'), 89
Cooke, S., 126
Corbridge, Nthumb. (view of A68 north of) **56**
Corrstown, Co. Londonderry, 27
Council for British Archaeology, 11
Crane, J., 103
Cron, F., 108
Crowthorne, Berks. **1**, **68**
Cugnot, N. (first steam-powered vehicle), 134
Cumbrian Hills, **2**
Cunliffe, B., 11, 27, **8**
cycling,
    hey-day of, 139
    on Devil's Highway, **68**
    opening of first section of National Cycle Network, **69**

Danebury hillfort, Hants., 25, 27, 155, **8**
Davies, G., 12
Davies, H., 13, 30, 40, 42, 78, 85, 90, 98, 121
deformation of soil (elastic and plastic), 75
Department for Transport, 11
Dere Street, 40
    line of A68 north of Corbridge, Nthumb., **56**
Devereux, P., 37
Devil's Highway, 40, **1**, **68**
Devil's Staircase, Glencoe, Highland Region, 61, **27**, **28**, *front cover*
Dover, Kent 29, 33, 41
droveways, 154
    Fengate, Cambs., 25
    Flag Fen, Cambs. **6**
    S. Hornchurch, Essex, 25, 154, **7**
Druids, 32
Dublin (link with London), 61

Eastbourne, Sussex 29
Edinburgh (Boswell's journey to London), 146
Edmonds, M., 32
Edwards, G., 96, **46**
Elder, J., 11
Elsevier Publishing, 11
enclosure, 31, 58
    layout of roads, 58
    North and South Killingholm, Lincs., **25**
Ermin Street, 46, 52
Ermine Street, 33, 46

Farnham, Surrey, 29
flagstones (use in road-making), 90
Folkstone, Kent 29
Fort Augustus (Highland Region), 60
Fort William, Highland Region, 61
    fort at, 60
Foss Way, 33, 40
    naming of, 47
    width of in Roman times, 78
Fowler, P., 31
Freeman, M., 130, 133, **65**

INDEX

freight movement: packhorse or wagon? 132
Frere, S., 80
Fulford, M., 11, 27, 78

Gallagher, W., 114, 116
Gantz, J., 35
Garrod, D., 21
Geoffrey of Monmouth, 33
Gerhold, D., 132
Glencoe, Highland Region, **27, 28**
    military road through, 61
Gloucester, 42, 46, 50, 52, 99, 110
    experiments with tarmacadam, 88
Godwin, F., 31
Goldcliff, Gwent, 20, 21
Golden Age of the stage coach, 130
Goring, Berks., 30
Gough Map, 32, 48, 99, 156, **17**
    missing sections of road, 50
Great Glen, Highland Region, 60
Great North Road, 50
    in turnpike era, 53
    Metcalf competes on foot with carriage, 126
    Stamford, Lincs. **18**
    travel times, 146
Great West Road, London, 136
Grimes, W., 29
Guest, E., 33
Guttmann, E., 25

Hadrian's Wall, 42
Hancock, W. (steam-powered passenger vehicle operation), 135
Harrison, D., 98, 99
Harrison, S., 31, 32
Hart, H., 131
Haslam, J., 47
Hay-on-Wye, Powys, 36
Helen of the Hosts, 35, 155
Henry of Huntington, 33
Herbert, Col. H., 151
Hereford, 36
Higden, R., 33
High Wycombe, Bucks., 99
Highways Agency, 144
Higman, D., 139
Hiller, J., 79
Hindle, P., 11, 30
Hobhouse, G., 11
Hogg, G., 83, 126
hollow-ways, 22, 80
Holme, Norfolk, 30
Holyhead Road, **33, 34**
    gradient of, 107
    loss of horses by the riding post, 62
    need for improvement of, 62, 63
    width of, 112
Hooke, D., 47
horses (number used in transport), 133
House of Lochar Publishing, 11
Howth, Ireland (harbour at), 61
Huddard, J. (Holyhead Road), 61
Huxford, R., 11

Icknield Way, 30, 31, 33, 46
Inglis, H., 110
Institution of Civil Engineers (ICE) 12, **43, 44, 45, 55, 60, 73, 74**
Inverness, Highland Region (fort at), 60

James VI of Scotland, 59
Jefferey, S. **40**
Johnson, C. **7**
juggernaut (coming of), 140
Jusserand, J., 100, 146

Kain, R., 58
Kemmis Betty, P., 12
Kennerell, E., 82
Killingholm (North and South), Lincs., **25**
King's Peace (violation of near Stafford), 146
Kinghouse, Highland Region, 61, **31**
Kingston, Surrey (bridge), 50
Kinlochleven, Highland Region, 61

Lake End Road West, Bucks., 79
Lamb, S., 11
Lancaster, O. (cartoons of 'by-pass varigated'), 150
Last, J., 25
Laurence, R., 11
Law, H., 85, 108, 112, 113
Lay, M., 82, 113
Leeds, 72
    motorway links to, 70
Leicester, 41, 42
ley lines, 19, 36, 37, 154
Lincoln, 41
    Roman concrete road, 89
Liverpool (motorway links to), 70
Living Streets (formerly Pedestrians Association), 11, 128, **62, 63**
Llandovery, Carms., 36
Llanfair Talhaiarn, Conway, **55**
Llansaran, Conway, **55**
Local Government Board, 54
Loch Ness, Highland Region, 61
London, 42, 50, 78, 133
    attitudes to developments on Western Avenue, 149
    Boswell's journey from Edinburgh, 146
    link with Dublin, 61
    motorway links to, 70
    proportion of journeys made on foot, 126
    rebuilding of arterials, 136
Lovat, Lord S., 59
Luttrell-type carriage, 129
Lutyens, Sir E., 71, 139

Mabinogion, The, 35
MacBride, D., 11
Macneill, Sir H., 107, **54**
Magor Pill, Gwent, 20
Maidenhead, Berks. (bridge), 50
Manchester,
    Middleton Road, **43, 44, 45**
    motorway links to, 70
Margary, I., 30, 40
Margate Pier, Kent, 88

Marlborough, Wilts., 50
Marples, M., 128
Martin, G., 145
Matthews, M., 11, **14**
McAdam, J., 86
    association of name with road-making, 87
    career, 85
    road-making technique, 85, 157
    specified by McAdam for Bristol to Bath road, 112
McGowan, C., 134
medieval roads (course of), 47
Mesolithic footprints, 13, 20, 154
Mesolithic period, 19
Metcalf, J. (Blind Jack of Knaresborough), 83
    on foot, in competition with carriage, 126
    rescuing people from drowning, 145
    use of brushwood foundation, 84
Michell, J., 35, 37
military roads in Scottish Highlands, **27**, **28**, **29**, **30**, **31**
    extent of, 61
    map of, **26**
    origin of, 59
Millar, T., 29
Morley, F., 146
motor roads,
    early development of, 69
    use of tolls, 160
motor vehicles,
    early twentieth century, 135
    first petrol-driven, 134
    legal definition of, 143
    limit on speed, 135
    limits on weight, 137
    lorries, 140
    number of, 136, 137, 158
    steam power in nineteenth century, 135
Motorway Archive Trust, 73
motorways,
    design speed, 116
    extent of in 1978, **35**
    highway link design method, 119
    in urban areas, 71
    M1, 70, 116, **58**
    M25, 71
    M4, 71, 116, **59**
    M5, 70
    M6, 70, **2**
    M74, **36**
    need for coordination of curves, 117
    urban (artist's impression of), **37**
Museum of London, 11

National Cycle Network, 139, **69**
Neolithic period, 19
Newbury, Berks., 72
Newcastle upon Tyne, 41

O'Connor, C., 98
Office of Public Service Information (formerly HMSO), 11
Ogilby, J. (maps by), 48
Old Ford, Essex, 78
Old Sarum, Wilts., 33

Oliver, R., 58
Onich, Highland Region, 61
Owselbury, Hants., 24
Oxford, 50
    attitudes to development on A40, 150

Paris, M. (maps by), 33, 48, **11**
Parnell, Sir H., 62
Parsons, E., 48
passenger and freight movement in S. Hants. **65**
Pastons (letters of), 133
Pawson, E., 54, **20**
Peddie, J., 42
Pedestrian Association (see Living Streets)
pedestrians, on Holland Park Avenue, London **64**
Pepys, S., 126
Perehinec, L., 12
Petts, D., 79
Philip, B., 21
Phillimore Publishing, 11
Pierce, P., 102
Piggott, S., 130
pitching, 84
Platt, E., 150
Pollard, J., 100
Porter, J., 12, 73, 98, 110, 113, 114, 116, 119, **57**, **61**
portland cement (invention of), 90
postal service (origin of), 133
Priestley-Bell, G., 11
Pryor, F., 21, 25
Puddlehill, Herts.,
    cutting at, **53**
    diversion of turnpike at, **21**

Quarry Products Association, 12
Quartermaine, J., 112

railways,
    impact on freight movements, 133
    impact on passenger travel, 130
Rakham, J., 21, **3**
Ravenglass, Cumbria, 41
Reader, W., 85
Reading, Berks., 50
    motorway links to, 71
Red Flag Act, 135
Rennie, J.,
    alleged contempt for road-building, 62
    Holyhead Road, 61
ribbon development, 150
Ridgeways, 20, 29, 32, 155, **10**
rise in street level,
    avoidance by modern practice, 82, **42**
    medieval period, 82
    Roman period, 78
River Severn, 20
road camber: crossfall and superelevation, 113
road capacity (limit of), 158, 159
road curvature,
    medieval, 115
    motor roads and motorways, 116
    Roman, 114
    transition curves, 116

INDEX

road geometry,
    curves on M4, **59**
    grade separation, 121, **61**
    poor coordination on autobahn, **60**
    straight section of M1, **58**
    transition curves, 116
road gradient,
    Birdlip Hill, Glos., 110
    cutting at Puddlehill, Herts., **53**
    definition and significance of, 105
    Llanfair Talhaiarn–Llansaran road, Conway, **55**
    motor roads, 110
    Telford's approach to, 107, **54**
road junctions,
    grade separation, 121, **61**
    Roman Pompeii and London, 121
    traffic flow, 119
road metalling,
    disagreement between Telford and McAdam, 85, 86
    drying by evaporation, 112
    eighteenth and nineteenth centuries, 82
    flexible or rigid? 94
    full-scale trials, 93
    High Street, Sandhurst, Berks. **47**, **48**
    Iron Age, 27, 77, 156
    layers of, **38**
    macadamised surfaces, 87, 110, 157, **23**
    Manchester (Middleton Road), **43**, **44**, **45**
    medieval period, 80, 82, **41**
    minor roads, variable strength of, 95, **46**
    modern, 90, 158, *Table* **1**
    planing machine, **42**
    Roman, 77, 156, **39**, **40**
    soil strength (importance of), 93
    tar and tarmacadam, 87, 157
    Telford's approach, 84
    watering, 87
Road Research Laboratory (RRL), 92
road safety, 144
    before the motor age, 145
    dangerous section of A68, **56**
    fatalities per vehicle, 149, 159
    motor age, 146
    number of fatalities, 1870-2000, **72**
road width, 111
    specified by McAdam, 112
Rolt, L., 61
Roman roads,
    course of, 40
    Dere Street, **16**
    early, 41
    Ermine Street, 53
    Gask Ridge, Perthshire, **15**
    map of, **9**, **12**, **13**
    names of, 46
    strategic planning, 156
Royal Roads, The Four, 19, 33, 48, 155
Royston, Herts., 53
Russell, R., 11, **25**
Ryknield (or Ryknild) Street, 46

Sainsbury's (use of horse-drawn vehicles), 137
Salisbury, G., 82

Salter, R., 93
Sandhurst, Berks., **47**, **48**
Sarn (Celtic origin of name), 47
Sarn Helen 47
Scales, R., 20
Scema Britannie 33, **11**
sedan chairs, 131
setts (use in road-making), 90
Shap Fell, Cumbria, **19**
Shrewsbury, Salop., 62, 64
Silchester Town Life Project, 11
Silchester, Hants., 27, 41, 42, 50, 155, **14**
    thickness of road at North Gate, 78
Slough, Berks.,
    motorway links to, 71
Smith, A., 54
Southwark (Thames crossing at), 42, 102
speed (limits on), 135
Sprey, J., 126
St Albans, 33, 42
Staines, Surrey (Roman crossing of the Thames at), 50
Stamford, Lincs., 50, **18**
Stane Street,
    excavation on, **40**
Stanegate (Norse origin of name), 47
Starkie, D., 73, **35**
steam-powered road vehicles, 69, 133
Stenton, Sir F., 48
Stirling, Aberdeenshire, 61
Stonehenge, Wilts., 31, 32
Stow, S., 11, 80
street audit, **63**
Sullivan, D., 37
Sunley, T., 12
SUSTRANS, 11, 140, **69**
Swindon, Wilts. (motorway links to), 71

tar (use of in road-making), 87
tarmacadam (tarmac), 69, 81
    coated, 88
    grouted, 88
    origin of name, 87
Taylor, C., 24, 31
Taylor, S., 131
Taylor, W., 60, **26**
Telford, T.,
    approach to gradient, 107, **54**
    career, 84
    Holyhead Road, 64, **33**, **34**
    Menai Bridge, 64, **32**
    road-making technique, 84, 157
    roads in Scottish Highlands, 59, 61
    width of Holyhead Road, 112
Tempus Publishing, 12
Thomas Telford Publishing, 12
Thomas, C., 21, **3**
Thorn, A., 37
timber trackways,
    Bramcote Green, Bermondsey, 21, 154, **3**
    Flag Fen, Cambs., 21, **4**, **5**
    Goldcliff, Newport, 21
    Greenwich, London, 21
    Sweet Track, Somerset, 21

Timmins, G., 110
Timperley, H., 29
Tomalin, C., 126
tons (conversion to tonnes), 143
Totnes, Devon, 33
trade (Prehistoric period), 32
trams, 126, 133, 147
Transport Research Laboratory (TRL), 92
    full-scale trials, 92
travel modes, 125
    freight movement: packhorses or wagons? 132
    on a horse or in a carriage, 129
    on foot, 126
    riding a bicycle, 139
Trevithick, R.,
    experiment on powered wheels, 134
    first powered road vehicle, 134
    first rail locomotive, 134
    high-pressure steam boiler, 134
turnpikes, 53, 59
    Abington, Lanarkshire, **23**, **24**
    extent of network, 54, **20**
    first toll-gate, 54
    reduction in travel times, 54, **22**
    resistance to tolls, 54, 146
Twyford, Berks., 87

University College, Lampeter, 11
Uskmouth, Gwent, 20

vehicle licenses, number of,
    1900-1940, **66**
    1900-2000, **67**
    commercial, 1900-2000, **70**
vehicle numbers,
    views of Elborough Street, London, 1900 and 2000, **73**, **74**

Wade, Major-Gen. G., 59, 61
wagon design (improvement in), 133
walk through the woods, **75**
walking, 126
Wall, Staffs., 50
Wansford, Cambs., 50
Wardens of Merton College (travel in medieval times), 145
Watkins, A., 36
Watling Street (West), 46
Watling Street, 33, 40, 46, 50, **21**
    origin of name, 46
    width of in Roman times, 78
Webb, B., 53
Webb, S., 53
weight of vehicles (limit on), 137, 142, **71**
Welsh Marches, 42, 46, 54
Western Avenue, London,
    rebuilding of, 136
Westhampnett, Sussex, **40**
wheels (width of), 143
White, M., 12
Williamson, T., 37
Winchester, Hants., 29
Wordsworth, D. and W. (walking), 128
Wright, C., 29, 31
Wroxeter, Salop, 41
Wynn, J., 137
Wynns (use of horse-drawn vehicles), 137

Yates, D., 11, 25, **7**
York, 41

zebra crossing (early example of), **62**

If you are interested in purchasing other books published by Tempus,
or in case you have difficulty finding any Tempus books in your local bookshop,
you can also place orders directly through our website

www.tempus-publishing.com